In the Name of Humanity

AMERICAN RELIEF AID IN GREECE, 1918–1929

The American School of Classical Studies at Athens gratefully acknowledges the support of the following individuals in the production of this volume:

Constantine (Deno) Macricostas
Zoë Sarbanes Pappas
Phokion Potamianos

Library of Congress Cataloging-in-Publication Data

Names: Daleziou, Eleftheria, editor. | Georgopoulou, Maria, editor. | Vogeikoff-Brogan, Natalia, editor.
Title: In the name of humanity : American relief aid in Greece, 1918-1929 / edited by Eleftheria Daleziou, Maria Georgopoulou, Natalia Vogeikoff-Brogan.
Description: Princeton, New Jersey : American School of Classical Studies at Athens, [2025] | Includes bibliographical references.
Identifiers: LCCN 2024057764 | ISBN 9780876619704 (paperback)
Subjects: LCSH: Humanitarian assistance, American–Greece–History–20th century–Exhibitions. | Food relief, American–Greece–History–20th century–Exhibitions. | Americans–Greece–Exhibitions. | Greece–History–1917-1944–Exhibitions. | Gennadius Library–Catalogs.
Classification: LCC HV555.G8 I6 2025 | DDC 949.507/2–dc23/eng/20250123
LC record available at https://lccn.loc.gov/2024057764

Printed in Italy

In the Name of Humanity

AMERICAN RELIEF AID IN GREECE, 1918–1929

EDITED BY

ELEFTHERIA DALEZIOU
MARIA GEORGOPOULOU
NATALIA VOGEIKOFF-BROGAN

AMERICAN SCHOOL OF CLASSICAL STUDIES AT ATHENS

ORGANIZATION
American School of Classical Studies at Athens

TEXTS
Eleftheria Daleziou (E.D.)
Jack L. Davis (J.L.D.)
Maria Georgopoulou (M.G.)
Christopher C. King (C.C.K.)
Armen T. Marsoobian (A.T.M.)
Yiorgo Topalidis (Y.T.)
Natalia Vogeikoff-Brogan (N.V.B.)

GRAPHIC DESIGN
Andreas Georgiadis

TRANSLATION
Sotiris Lappas

TEXT EDITING
Leda Costaki, Jack L. Davis,
Antonia Gounaropoulou

WITH SPECIAL THANKS

Vasilis Alexopoulos
Kalliopi Amygdalou
Jenny Barker-Devine
Ryan Bean
Nikos Chrissidis
Jack L. Davis
Paul-Marinos Delladetsimas
Maria Dimitriadou
Paul Farnham
Andonis Godis
Molly Haigh
Vilma Hastaoglou-Martinidis
Matthew Herbison
Roger Jennings
Christopher C. King
Ioanna Klavdianou
Elisavet Komninou
Damiana Koutsomiha
Ismene Lamb
Panayotis League
Charis Liapi
George Manginis
April Michas
Demetra Papaconstantinou
Ioannis Papadopoulos
Renee Pappous
Jennifer Sacher
Tassos Sakellaropoulos
Aggeliki Saplaoura
Julia L. Shear
Shannan Stewart
Sharon R. Stocker
Vahé Tachjian
Scott S. Taylor
Evi Tramantza
Aliki Tsirgialou
Lou Ureneck
Toni Vanden Bos
George Veranis
Alexandra Vovolini
Chris Wydman
Lefteris Zorzos

American College of Greece Archives and Special Collections

American Farm School Historical Archives

Anatolia College Archives and Special Collections – Trustees of Anatolia College

Athens Law Group

Benaki Museum Historical Archives

Benaki Museum Photographic Archives

Booth Family Center for Special Collections, Georgetown University Library, Washington, D.C.

ERT Archives (Hellenic Radio and Television)

Estias Neas Smyrnis

General State Archives of Greece

Kautz Family YMCA Archives, University of Minnesota Libraries

Khalaf Al Habtoor Archives, Illinois College, Jacksonville, Illinois

Legacy Center Archives and Special Collections, Drexel University College of Medicine

Library of Congress, Prints and Photographs Division, Washington, D.C.

Museum of Pharmacology, Medical School of Athens

Naval History and Heritage Command, Washington, D.C.

Near East Relief Project

Newberry Library, Chicago

Ottoman Greeks of the U.S. Digital History Project, University of Florida

Rockefeller Archive Center , Sleepy Hollow, N.Y.

UCLA, Library Special Collections, Charles E. Young Research Library

University of Washington Libraries, Special Collections

Wright State University Libraries, Special Collections and Archives

Yarmouth County Museum and Archives

Contents

Greek and Armenian orphans near Athens, 1923. (Library of Congress, Prints and Photographs Division, Washington, D.C.)

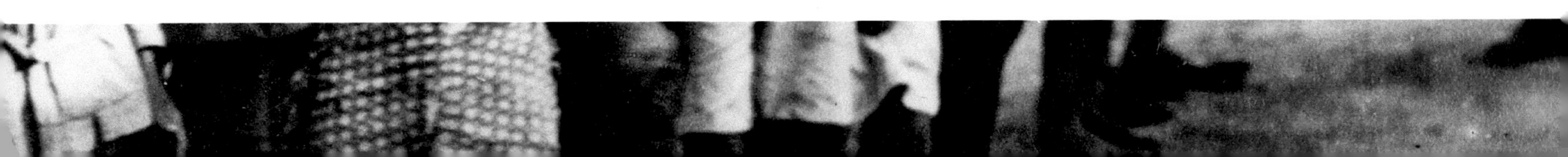

Children in a refugee camp, ca. 1922–1923. (George Horton Papers, Booth Family Center for Special Collections, Georgetown University Library, Washington, D.C.)

Foreword

Bonna Wescoat
Director of the American School of Classical Studies at Athens

The American School of Classical Studies at Athens is proud to open the exhibition *In the Name of Humanity: American Relief Aid in Greece, 1918–1929*, which draws on the rich collections of the Archives and the Gennadius Library to create a powerfully evocative narrative of the relief efforts made by Americans to support refugees in Greece throughout the turbulent years following World War I.

I heartily thank the curators of the exhibition, Eleftheria Daleziou, Maria Georgopoulou, and Natalia Vogeikoff-Brogan, for bringing together personal papers, posters, photographs, films, and artifacts that offer new insights into American involvement in this critical period of Greek and world history. The exhibition balances the efforts of organizations, such as the American Red Cross, the Near East Relief, and the American Women's Hospitals, with the pivotal roles played by intrepid individuals, particularly women, who served as doctors, nurses, educators, and advocates.

The aim to create opportunity through education was a fundamental part of American humanitarian aid, as witnessed by the relocation of Anatolia College to Thessaloniki and the American Collegiate Institute for Girls in Smyrna, which reopened in Athens as the American Junior College for Girls. The American Farm School in Thessaloniki expanded to serve the needs of orphan refugees.

American companies responded to the need to develop fundamental resources, such as water supply and land reclamation, to accommodate the influx of refugees. Designed and built by Americans working side by side with some 900 refugees from Asia Minor, the Marathon Dam, which still serves Athens, is a product of this period.

The exhibition also brings to light the involvement of key figures associated with the American School. The personal papers of Bert H. Hill and Carl W. Blegen (persons well known for their contributions to Greek archaeology) reveal their deep involvement in relief efforts. Edward Capps, chair of the School's Managing Committee, headed the Greek Commission of the American Red Cross, and when that organization withdrew from Greece, he founded the American Friends of Greece. Capps's daughter, Priscilla, created the Near East Industries in Athens, which crafted and sold dolls in folk costumes, purses, and embroideries, to create income for the refugee women. At just this time, Joannes Gennadius donated his library to the American School of Classical Studies to form the foundational core of the Gennadius Library and become the cornerstone around which thriving post-antique investigations have been built over the last century.

The Board of Trustees of the American School of Classical Studies and the Overseers of the Gennadius Library have been steadfast in their support of this exhibition. Their encouragement and financial backing have been critical to its success. As always, we appreciate their vibrant commitment to the mission of the American School.

In the Name of Humanity centers on the Greek refugee crisis during 12 critical years in the early 20th century. A century later, we are not strangers to similar crises. It is good to be reminded of how others—not so very different from us—rose to meet the challenges of those in need. The several American groups and individuals involved in relief aid to Greece were compelled by various missions, but their aims at heart were humanitarian. Schools, hospitals, orphanages, waterworks, and land reclamation are the tangible marks of American efforts to aid refugees and Greece in coping with the crisis. But the far greater legacy lies in the many people who are with us today because their immediate ancestors had the strength, courage, and resilience to survive and thrive when help, in large and small ways, was made available. We hold this exhibition in recognition of them and of all who assisted along the way.

George Orfanakos's great grandparents and maternal grandmother, Catherine Pavlides Karakizes (far right), and her siblings, prior to their departure from Asia Minor, ca. 1921. (Personal collection of George Orfanakos)

Crisis, Compassion, and Courage

George Orfanakos
Executive Director of the American School of Classical Studies at Athens

Throughout history, there are moments that capture both the darkest and brightest aspects of humanity. The *In the Name of Humanity* exhibition sheds light on one such period, highlighting the extraordinary philanthropic response of the U.S. to the humanitarian crisis following the Asia Minor Catastrophe.

The scholars at the American School of Classical Studies at Athens have meticulously researched and brought to life the remarkable efforts that arose during this challenging time. The exhibition recounts how men, women, and children faced destruction, despair, and death as they entered a country already struggling to care for its own people, let alone a massive influx of refugees.

Yet, amidst the turmoil, a beacon of hope emerged from afar. Strangers from a distant land answered the call for support, offering philanthropic contributions that saved countless lives. Generations owe their existence to this generosity and the selfless actions of those who extended a helping hand. I know this firsthand, as I am a descendant of those refugees. I live each day with profound gratitude, understanding that if others had not come to their aid, I might never have been born.

Over several years, these displaced individuals faced the daunting task of finding new homes, sustaining their lives, and rebuilding from nothing. This monumental challenge required the support and solidarity of many, and it was not an endeavor they could undertake alone.

A crucial aspect of this narrative is the role of women in ensuring the survival of their families. In the face of overwhelming adversity, when many men succumbed to depression and despair, it was often the women who stood resilient. They became the pillars of strength, guiding their families through the darkest hours and illuminating the path forward.

As we reflect on this story, we hope that such dark moments in history will never be repeated. However, as refugee crises continue to exist today, the humanitarian response exemplified in this exhibition serves as a powerful reminder of the impact we can have on others. Let this story inspire us to act with compassion and humanity, recognizing the profound difference we can make in the lives of those in need.

Distribution of clothing to refugee children by the American Red Cross, ca. 1923. (Library of Congress, Prints and Photographs Division, American National Red Cross Photograph Collection)

In the Name of Humanity

Eleftheria Daleziou, Maria Georgopoulou,
and Natalia Vogeikoff-Brogan

When the whole story of this work [humanitarian relief] is written, it will take pride of place as a glorious page in the annals of mankind, and its charity will shine like a brilliant star in a long and dark night. At the same time, the Americans have, through other organizations such as the American Red Cross and the Near East Relief, achieved the unbelievable in the Balkans, in Asia Minor, and now, finally in Greece.
—Fridtjof Nansen, "The Suffering People of Europe"
Nobel Prize Lecture, December 19, 1922

On the centenary of the signing of the Lausanne Convention, the American School of Classical Studies at Athens (ASCSA or American School hereafter) presents an exhibition spotlighting a monumental humanitarian endeavor etched in history: the American relief aid extended to Greece between 1918 and 1929.

The profound impact of the Lausanne Convention's population exchange reverberated for a decade as 1.2 million Greek Orthodox Turkish nationals were uprooted from Turkey to Greece, while 400,000 Greek nationals of the Muslim religion were moved from Greece to Turkey. This pivotal moment summoned the benevolent efforts of several esteemed American humanitarian agencies—including the American Red Cross, the Near East Relief, the American Women's Hospitals, and the Young Men's Christian Association (YMCA)—which united to deliver invaluable emergency relief to orphaned children and displaced refugees. Furthermore, these organizations, in collaboration with the American Friends of Greece, the American Collegiate Institute Relief Committee, and the Near East Industries, ingeniously orchestrated avenues for employment, foundational education, and comprehensive mental and physical healthcare. These multifaceted initiatives empowered the refugees, particularly women, by providing them with necessary tools and resources to attain self-sufficiency, thus fostering resilience and rejuvenation within their lives.

This exhibition brings into focus the tireless efforts of diverse individuals, ranging from political appointees and philanthropic leaders to educators and dedicated relief workers. Motivated by a sense of duty rooted in Christian, patriotic, or personal beliefs, they collectively played a pivotal role in reshaping Greece after 1922. The exhibition draws on a rich array of resources, including correspondence, official documents, rare publications, photographs, artifacts, posters, short films, and handmade crafts. These treasures, curated from the extensive collections of the ASCSA and borrowed from various institutions, converge here for the first time to weave a compelling narrative of profound significance.

Bert H. Hill, Carl W. Blegen, Edward Capps and his daughter Priscilla, and Joannes Gennadius were key figures associated with the American School, and each played a crucial role in U.S. relief aid to Greece. They were the connecting tissue between Greece and America in more than one way, serving as conduits for American involvement in Greece in the interwar period. Hill, director of the American School for 20 years (1906–1926), was well regarded and had high-profile connections, especially with the Greek royal family. He described himself as an "adjuster and negotiator" and was instrumental in facilitating the work of the American Red Cross (ARC) in 1918 and 1919, in responding to the refugee crisis in 1922 by chairing the Athens American Relief Committee, and later, in 1927, by serving as acting chairman of the Refugee Settlement Commission. His personal papers in the ASCSA Archives include extensive documentation of his relief work, his tours of inspection in rural refugee settlements in Macedonia, and his involvement in a census of urban refugees.

Hill and Carl W. Blegen, the School's secretary, shared a deep knowledge of Greece (its geography, language, and customs) and both were already volunteering for the American Legation in Greece, ensuring that the Greek families of the 2,500 Greek American soldiers on World War I battlefields were receiving compensation. We would not have known much about Blegen's service with the ARC in typhus-ridden Eastern Macedonia without his own diary (on display) of his service in the first half of 1919. Blegen's mission was to organize the repatriation of thousands of Greeks who had been taken hostage to Bulgaria.

One thing is for certain: without Hill and Blegen on the ground, Edward Capps, the newly appointed chair of the School's Managing Committee (1918–1939), would not have headed the Greek Commission of the ARC. A professor of Classics at Princeton University, Capps became Minister to Greece during the last months of Woodrow Wilson's presidency (1920–1921). It is not clear when and how it was decided that he would lead the Greek Commission. The fact that he had been a colleague of Wilson's at Princeton must have played some role. That Capps had access to the American School, a repository of local experience, must have given him a leg up in the selection process. He should also be credited with the publication of the Commission's reports as separate booklets. As a scholar Capps knew the power of disseminating published documents. In 1919 the Greek government decorated Capps, Hill, and Blegen for their service with the ARC. Today only Hill's decoration is preserved in the ASCSA Archives (on display). Another object testifying to the American School's involvement with the ARC is a Singer sewing machine, which was rediscovered in the basement of the director's house. It carries a brass plaque: "CROCE ROSSA AMERICANA."

Capps continued to be concerned with Greek affairs long after 1919. Through his service with the ARC he had met Eleftherios Venizelos, and was widely viewed as a strong supporter of that Greek politician. On November 12, 1922, Capps published a long article in the *New York Times*, "$33,000,000 Due to Greece on Loan Held to Be Our Debt of Honor," holding the U.S. government accountable for Greece's financial collapse. In 1923, after the premature withdrawal of the ARC from Greece, Capps, together with other Americans who had firsthand knowledge of the situation, felt strongly that the Greek refugee problem was far from over. Capps acted by creating the American Friends of Greece (AFG). The organization's membership list included many important American philhellenes. In a series of press releases issued in early 1924, the AFG counteracted announcements by the ARC that the Greek refugee problem had been solved. Today only one of the organization's pamphlets is preserved in the ASCSA Archives, and its contribution to Greek affairs remains largely unknown.

Fortunately, we discovered an entire folder about the American Friends in the online catalogue of the League of Nations Archives in Geneva. Further research into the activities of the AFG and its association with the Greek American community in New York City will surely define even better the role that this organization played in shaping the opinion and the support of the diaspora, as even cursory exploration of the Greek American newspaper the *National Herald* suggests. We cannot emphasize enough the importance of having access to online resources, such as the photographic collections of the Library of Congress or photos of the YMCA in the National Documentation Center. This exhibition would not have been possible 10 to 15 years ago, and a large part of it is based on primary and unpublished research.

The incorporation of the AFG in 1923 marked the start of Priscilla Capps's involvement in refugee affairs. Priscilla had assisted her father, Edward Capps, in Athens during his service as U.S. Minister to Greece. In 1925 she moved to Greece to manage the embroidery workshops that the AFG had developed in Athens to support refugee women. Priscilla would make Greece her home until 1941 when she was forced to leave as the U.S. entered World War II. Her work with the Near East Industries, as the AFG Workshops rebranded themselves, also remains largely unknown. It was Jack Davis's preoccupation with Edward Capps that led him to discover Priscilla's activities. Since 2016 he has been systematically collecting products of the Near East Industries and donating them to the ASCSA Archives. Unknowingly, and by a fortunate coincidence, another member of the American School's extended family, April Michas, was collecting the handsome purses and embroideries that Priscilla's workshops produced. Both collections, together with a third recently gifted to the ASCSA Archives by Julia L. Shear and Alexandra Shear, form part of this exhibition. We thank them all.

Further research on the Near East Industries could not but lead to the activities of the parent organization, the Near East Relief (NER). A series of posters produced in 1919 to support a $30 million campaign of the NER introduces the visitor to its work with Armenian and Syrian refugees before 1922. We are also privileged to have in the American School the personal papers of Dorothy H. Sutton, who joined the NER overseas personnel in 1920, working first in Turkey and, after 1922, managed NER orphanages set up in Greece. It so happened that on the premises of the NER orphanage on Syros, pieces of garments, kitchen utensils, and the toys of the orphans were discovered. We are grateful to Lefteris Zorzos for lending us some of these items for our exhibition. Alice G. Carr, another NER worker and nurse, is remembered for her pivotal work in Corinth fighting malaria.

Studying Sutton's career and trying to understand how the Near East Relief operated in Greece allowed us to highlight the work of the many American women who volunteered in Greece in the interwar period, including Olga Stastny and Ruth Parmelee, doctors at the American Women's Hospitals. Both organizations long continued to operate in Greece, supporting initiatives in health care and vocational education, and maintaining hospitals and health centers. Their work remains almost unknown in Greece, so the exhibition highlights these brave women, who put their spirit, heart, and life at the service of more than one million distressed refugees.

In 1922 Joannes Gennadius, a noted Greek diplomat who had lobbied extensively for Greece in England and the U.S., decided to bequeath his cherished collection of 30,000 volumes to the American School. "This gift forged a new robust and unbroken bond with Greece in order to benefit its national interests," Gennadius wrote. Indeed, the Gennadius Library was the first major library in Greece to focus on the study of the Byzantine, post-Byzantine, and modern Greek world; it was a library embodying the ideology of the "Megali Idea" that was built on its ashes by destitute refugees, thanks to the generosity of the Carnegie Corporation. It is no accident that it was Edward Capps who encouraged Gennadius to make this gift in order to broaden the educational scope and agenda of the American School.

Hand in glove with U.S. humanitarian aid to Greece, Greek American commercial relations expanded considerably in the 1920s. American endeavors such as the construction of the Marathon Dam and the reclamation of the Strymon and Drama valleys marked transformative milestones in Greece's infrastructure. These projects not only provided employment opportunities for vulnerable refugees but also ushered in an improved quality of life, devoid of the scourges of malaria and disease.

Malaria and disease were also part and parcel of relief efforts by American educational institutions along with their educational, athletic, and recreational activities. The American Farm School (founded in Thessaloniki in 1904) became a true incubator for young farmers by introducing to Macedonia many technological innovations, from the straight-tooth harrow, the cultivator, and the tractor to a model meteorological station. The American Junior College for Girls, which transferred its seat from Smyrna to Athens, opened many academic and professional opportunities for young women, who were encouraged to excel in the classroom and beyond. Run by missionaries, some of these institutions were seen with suspicion in Greece owing to the strict Greek laws against proselytizing. Still, they inspired confidence in the population. As Anatolia College President George E. White noted, "in spite of impoverishment, bereavement and exile, the people plan and plead for the education of their boys."

The interwar period was a turbulent time for Greek education as the Venizelists were pushing for a secular and liberal schooling away from the prescriptions of the Church. The welcoming of several American schools to Greek soil proved crucial for the modernization of Greek education by importing tenets of the U.S. liberal arts colleges. So, beyond the committed relief efforts for refugees by the missionaries who ran them, the lasting legacies of these educational institutions are the thousands of their graduates who excelled in Greece or the U.S. as valuable members of their respective societies by displaying a robust work ethic.

This exhibition also accents Ottoman Greeks who embarked on a journey to America. They played a vital role, contributing to humanitarian aid efforts in support of their fellow countrymen in Greece, while simultaneously forging a distinctive identity on American shores. Recent research on the mutual aid societies that were formed by Greek Americans and Ottoman Greek migrants to the U.S. provides a new framework within which to appreciate identity formation in the diaspora. (The term "Ottoman Greek," referring to Greek Orthodox Turkish nationals, was coined by U.S. immigration authorities on Ellis Island.) Linguistic, racial, and cultural differences seemingly kept Greek and Ottoman Greek communities apart; we are only starting to understand these nuances through the pioneering research of Yiorgo Topalidis, whom we thank for his generosity in sharing his work with us.

The Greek American Anatolian diaspora made significant cultural contributions, notably through the widespread dissemination of folk and *rembetika* songs that captured the challenges of population exchange. These expressions vividly explore the profound impact of America on the refugees' lives. We are grateful to Christopher C. King for enriching this exhibition with his unique knowledge and with several items from his 78-rpm record collection, which capture the voices, rhythms, instruments, and above all the longing (καημός) of the refugees for their lost homelands.

This exhibition, like the topic that it covers, has been very much a collective effort. We owe immense gratitude to many colleagues who have come forward to assist with their erudition, family stories, personal experience, or collections. We would like to express our gratitude to George Mavrogordatos, William McGrew, and Antony Molho for fruitful discussions that have shaped or clarified many points that are treated herein.

The sections on the American Red Cross and the American Friends of Greece would not have been complete without the quinine containers from the Museum of Pharmacology of the Athens Medical School, for which we thank Ioannis Papadopoulos, and the Singer sewing machine, loaned to us by Elisavet Komninou. We are also grateful to Jenny Barker-Devine of Illinois College for facilitating access to the papers of Carl E. Black, one of the American Red Cross commissioners, and Renee Pappous of the Rockefeller Archive Center for supplying us with material from the archives of the Near East Relief.

We thank Kalliopi Amygdalou who shared her unique expertise on the urban configuration of refugee settlements in Athens, and Vilma Hastaoglou-Martinidi and Paul-Marinos Delladetsimas for material on the YMCA Palace in Thessaloniki, a work designed by Marinos Delladetsimas in the Byzantine style. Andonis Godis has been an invaluable source of information about the YMCA in Greece; we are deeply grateful for his willingness to support our project. We are grateful to Damiana Koutsomiha, head librarian at the Dimitris & Aliki Perrotis Library of the American Farm School and Perrotis College, who has bent over backward to assist us with loans from the American Farm School historical archives. We are indebted to Demetra Papaconstantinou, archivist of the American College of Greece Archives and Special Collections, who has offered her own research and expertise in the search for original material to highlight the first years of the American Junior College for Girls in Palaio Phaleron. We thank the Trustees of Anatolia College and especially Evi Tramantza, director of Libraries & Archives at Anatolia College, for all their help in providing us with information about the rich resources of this unique institution.

Our thanks go to colleagues in the U.S. who lent their time and effort in providing us with digital copies of photographic and archival material: Matthew Herbison of the Legacy Center Archives, Drexel University College of Medicine, holders of the American Women's Hospitals Archives; Chris Wydman and Toni Vanden Bos of the Wright State University Special Collections and Archives, for material on Alice G. Carr; Ryan Bean, archivist of the Kautz Family YMCA Archives at the University of Minnesota Libraries for material about the YMCA; and staff at the Navy Department Library, Naval History and Heritage Command. Ismene Lamb and Scott S. Taylor at Georgetown University have been extremely generous in locating and sharing material about George Horton.

Photograph from the Dourgouti refugee camp. (American College of Greece Archives and Special Collections)

Paul Farnham and Robert Jennings have allowed us to use photographs of their grandfathers Adelbert Bartlett and Asa K. Jennings, respectively.

The reliable and dedicated support of Maria Smali on all organizational aspects has been a reassuring force for the impeccable execution of every detail of the exhibition and we thank her profusely. Leda Costaki, Jack Davis, Jennifer Sacher, and Antonia Gounaropoulou contributed with their editing skills, and Sotiris Lappas with the Greek translation. The input of the Athens Law Group into the lending process was crucial.

We thank ASCSA director Bonna Wescoat for her support and advice throughout the project, as well as George Orfanakos and Joanne Berdebes, who have contributed significantly to the promotion of the project in the U.S.

Heartfelt thanks go to Andreas Georgiadis, Vivi Gerolymatou, and their team at Mikri Arktos for the inspired design and thorough execution of the exhibition and the catalogue.

Finally, this exhibition would not have happened without the generosity of Constantine (Deno) Macricostas and Zoë Sarbanes Pappas to whom we owe a debt of gratitude. Deno was born in the *American Women's Hospital* in Kokkinia in 1935. To Phokion Potamianos we are indebted immensely for financing the publication of this catalogue. The support and encouragement of the Overseers of the Gennadius Library under the leadership of Andreas Zombanakis, who has championed the celebration of this unique American humanitarian effort, set in motion the entire project. To them and the whole team of the American School, which helped us along every step of the way, we owe our gratitude.

Abbreviations

AARC: Athens American Relief Committee
ACG: American College of Greece
ACI: American Collegiate Institute for Girls
AFG: American Friends of Greece
ARC: American Red Cross
ASCSA: American School of Classical Studies at Athens
AWH: American Women's Hospitals
NEI: Near East Industries
NER: Near East Relief
NEF: Near East Foundation
YMCA: Young Men's Christian Association

Timeline

1914-18 World War I

1915 Ambassador Morgenthau informs the U.S. State Department about the "destruction of the Armenian race in Turkey"

Foundation of the American Committee for Armenian and Syrian Relief

1917 America enters the War. Greece declares war against the Central Powers

Foundation of American Women's Hospitals (AWH)

1918 Armistice of November 11 ends World War I

ACASR renamed as the American Committee for Relief in the Near East (ACRNE)

The Greek Commission of the American Red Cross (ARC) arrives in Greece

1919 ACRNE's $30 million campaign and incorporation as the Near East Relief (NER) by the U.S. Senate

1919–22 Greco-Turkish War. Greek army lands in Smyrna (1919)

1920 Treaty of Sèvres signed between the Allied Powers and the Ottoman Empire. Foundation of the League of Nations

1921 Foundation of the Young Men's Christian Association (YMCA) of Thessaloniki

1922 Asia Minor Catastrophe. Burning of Smyrna

The Athens American Relief Committee (AARC) and the American Collegiate Institute Relief Committee are established in Athens

Arrival of the ARC in Greece

Joannes Gennadius donates his personal library to the American School of Classical Studies at Athens

The Near East Relief (NER) transfers its base from Istanbul to Athens

American Women's Hospitals establishes its operation in Athens and the islands

1923 Lausanne Convention. Compulsory population exchange between Greece and Turkey

The ARC withdraws from Greece

Establishment of the Refugee Settlement Commission under Henry Morgenthau

Incorporation of the American Friends of Greece (AFG)

Relocation of Anatolia College from Merzifon to Thessaloniki

Foundation of the YMCA of Athens

Relocation of the American Collegiate Institute for Girls from Smyrna to Athens

1924 Establishment of the AFG Workshops

Greek government signs contract with Ulen & Company to build the Marathon Waterworks

Immigration Act in the U.S. introduces quotas to curtail immigration from the Near East

1926 The AFG Workshops become Near East Industries (NEI)

Dedication of the Gennadius Library

Anatolia College and the American College of Greece accredited by the Greek Ministry of Culture

1928 Reclamation of the Strymon and Drama valleys granted to John Monks & Sons and Ulen & Company

1929 American stock market crash. Beginning of the Great Depression

1930 The Near East Relief becomes the Near East Foundation (NEF)

1931 Inauguration of the Marathon Dam

Opposite: Photograph from the Dourgouti refugee camp. (American College of Greece Archives and Special Collections)

Dergouti

Dramatis Personae

James L. Barton
(1855–1936) Protestant missionary and educator. Chairman of the NER, 1919–1930

Carl W. Blegen
(1887–1971) Archaeologist and ASCSA officer. Attached to the ARC in Macedonia, 1919

Edward Capps
(1866–1950) Professor of Classics and chair of the ASCSA Managing Committee. ARC commissioner, 1918–1919, and chair of the AFG, 1923–1925

Priscilla Capps
(1900–1985) Director of the NEI Athens, 1926–1940

Alice G. Carr
(1887–1968) Nurse with the ARC and the NER, 1917–1929. Director of Public Health for the NEF, 1930–1948

Carl C. Compton
(1891–1982) Missionary, teacher, coach, and dean of Anatolia College, 1925–1939, and
Ruth Magavren Compton
(1892–1979) Missionary and NER worker

Sara Corning
(1872–1969) Nurse and NER worker in the Ottoman Empire and Greece, 1919–1930

Cleveland H. Dodge
(1860–1926) Businessman. Treasurer of the NER, 1915–1926

Florence Spencer Duryea
(1884–1966) Philanthropist and fundraiser for the NEF

Roy W. Gausmann
(1882–1974) Engineer and assistant manager of the Marathon Dam project. General manager of the Hellenic Water Company

Joannes Gennadius
(1844–1932) Diplomat and bibliophile

Darrell O. Hibbard
(1881–1948) Educator and director of the YMCA at Athens, 1920–1924

Bert H. Hill
(1874–1958) Archaeologist and ASCSA director, 1906–1926. Worked with the ARC, 1918–1919. Chairman of the AARC, 1922–1923

George Horton
(1859–1942) American consul general at Smyrna, 1911–1917, 1919–1920

John Henry House
(1845–1936) Founder and director of the American Farm School, 1904–1929, and
Susan Adeline Beers House
(1850–1947) Missionary and educator

Charles Lucius House
(1887–1961) Director of the American Farm School, 1929–1955, and
Ann Kellogg House
(1888–1989) Educator

Harold C. Jaquith
(1889–1943) Managing director of the NER in Constantinople and in Athens, 1921–1926. Associate general secretary of the NER, 1927–1929

Asa K. Jennings
(1877–1933) Missionary with the YMCA in Smyrna, 1922

Herbert Parker Lansdale Jr.
(1898–1988) General secretary of the YMCA at Thessaloniki, 1925–1931. National director of Greek YMCAs, 1927–1939

Esther P. Lovejoy
(1869–1967) Physician and public health pioneer, president of the AWH, 1919–1967

Emily McCallum
(1858–1956) Principal of the American College for Girls in Smyrna and Athens, 1893–1928

Minnie Mills
(1872–1965) Missionary, dean of the American Collegiate Institute in Smyrna and at Palaio Phaleron, 1895–1928. Principal of the American College for Girls in Athens, 1928–1932. President of the College, 1932–1940

Henry Morgenthau
(1856–1946) U.S. ambassador to the Ottoman Empire, 1913–1916

Ruth Azniv Parmelee
(1885–1973) Physician and missionary, member of the AWH in Greece, 1922–1941

Olga Stastny
(1878–1952) Physician and member of the NER and the AWH

Dorothy H. Sutton
(1878–1970) NER worker in the Ottoman Empire and Greece, 1920–1927

W. Stuart Thompson
(1890–1968) Architect of the Gennadius Library, 1926. Athens representative of the AFG, 1924–1925

Gladys Slade Thompson
(1889–1975) Athens representative of the AFG and supervisor of its workshops, 1924–1925

George E. White
(1861–1946) Missionary and president of Anatolia College, 1914–1933, and
Esther Burrill Robbins White
(1860–1950) Missionary and educator

George DeForest White
(1893–1969) Missionary and director of the NER orphanage in Syros, and general manager of Anatolia College, 1928–1939, and
Elsie Hoesley White
(1894–1960) Missionary at the NER orphanage

Charlotte Willard
(1860–1930) Principal of the Girls School and the School for the Deaf at Anatolia College in Merzifon and a NER worker, 1898–1929

Distribution of bread, Kavala, 1919. (Horace S. Oakley, *In Macedonia*, Chicago, 1920. ASCSA, Gennadius Library)

1

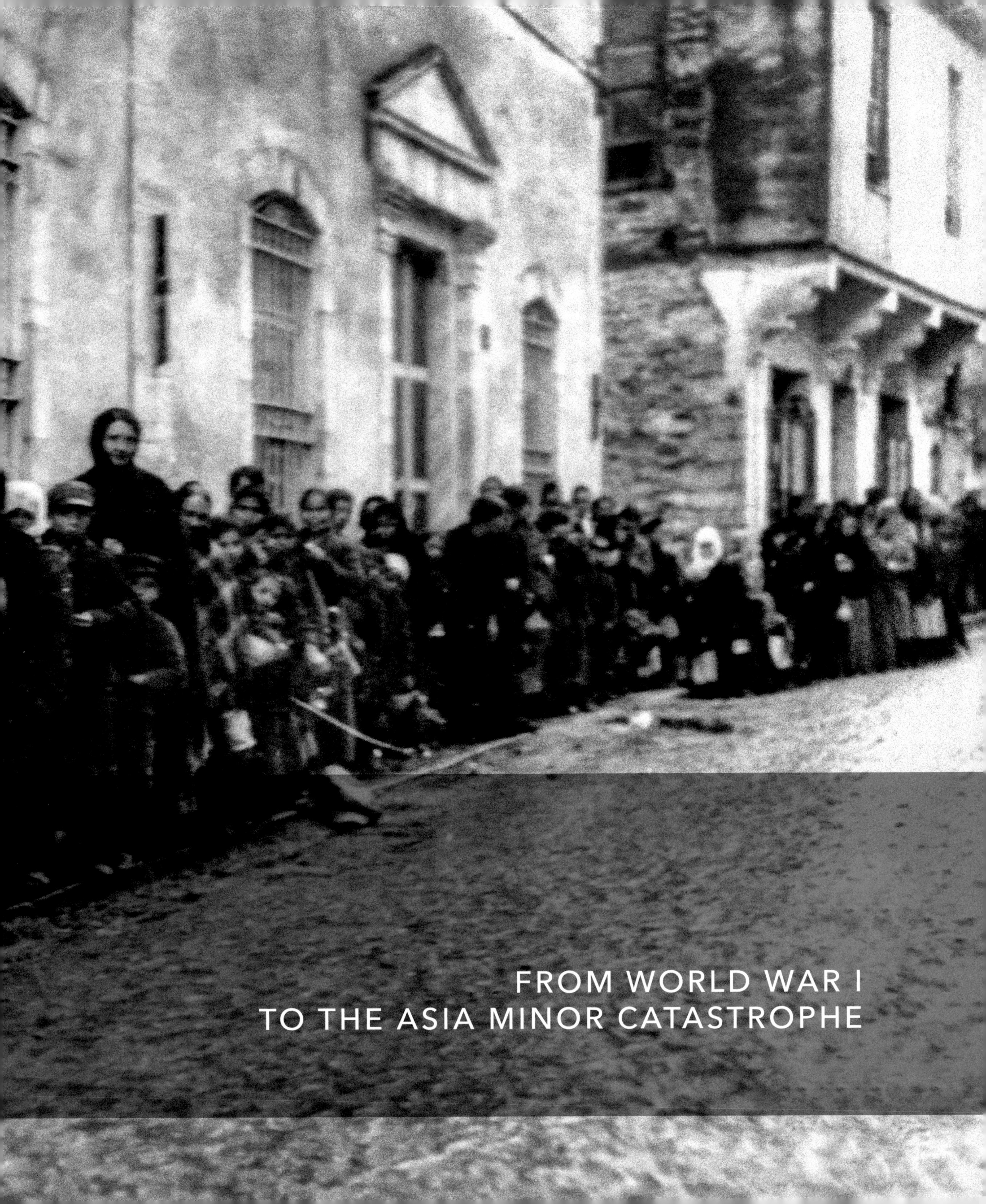

FROM WORLD WAR I
TO THE ASIA MINOR CATASTROPHE

Postcard of the ARC in Greece, 1919. (Khalaf Al Habtoor Archives, Illinois College, Jacksonville, Illinois, Carl E. Black Papers)

1A The American Red Cross in Greece, 1918–1919

After America entered the war in 1917, the American Red Cross (ARC), with the endorsement of President Woodrow Wilson, who was also the President of the ARC, sent several commissions to Europe to provide military and civilian relief. Although service in the ARC was not a substitute for combat, the militarization of the ARC after 1917 was viewed as an alternative form of service by many men who were beyond draft age. Businessmen, doctors, and professors became majors and lieutenant colonels overnight.

The ARC Greek Commission was organized in June 1918, in response to an appeal from the Greek Red Cross. It was headed by Edward Capps, professor of Classics at Princeton and a colleague of President Wilson. Moreover, Capps, as newly appointed chair of the Managing Committee of the American School of Classical Studies at Athens (ASCSA), had access to American staff and facilities in Athens. Bert H. Hill and Carl W. Blegen, director and secretary of the School, respectively, not only shared deep knowledge of Greece, but were also well connected with the local community.

From November 1918 until May 1919 the ARC Greek Commission operated in Eastern Macedonia, facilitating the repatriation of more than one hundred thousand Greeks who had been deported to Bulgaria in 1917, distributing food and clothes, and fighting a typhus epidemic. Another mission to Mytilene and the adjacent islands offered civilian relief to Greek refugees from Asia Minor following the Turkish expulsions of 1913–1914.

Apart from the work in Macedonia and the Northern Aegean islands, the Greek Commission offered general civilian relief in many places in Greece by establishing infant welfare stations, *ouvroirs* (sewing rooms), and a factory for a lighter type of prosthetics, and by conducting studies focused on the long-term improvement of agricultural production and hospital care.

The Greek Commission of the ARC left Greece in June 1919. Before that, many of its members were decorated by King Alexander.

N.V.B.

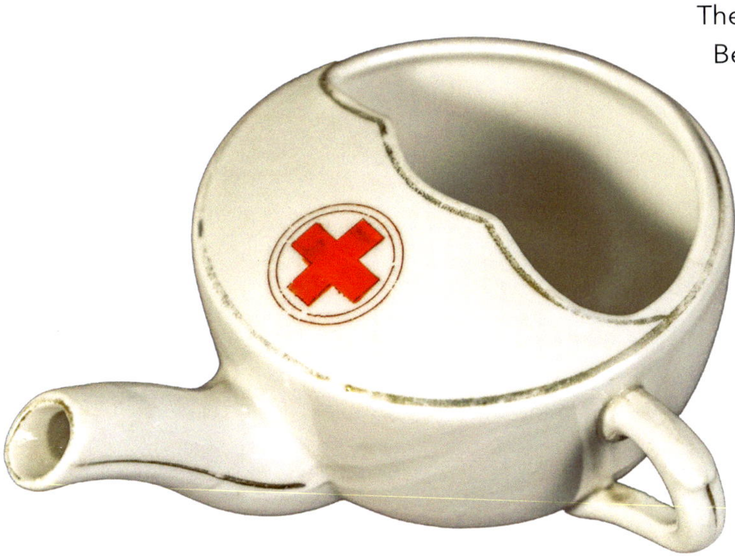

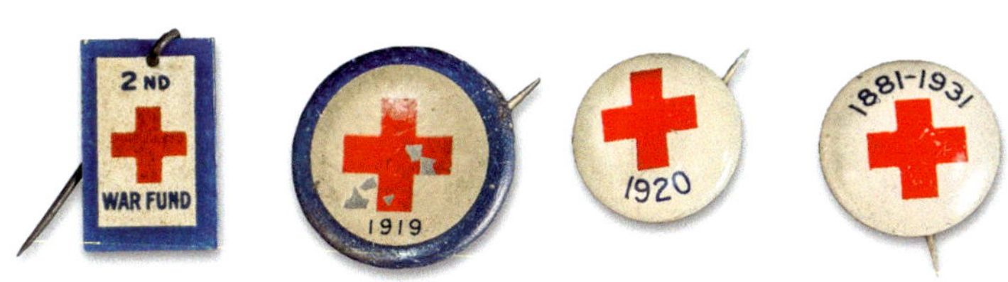

ARC feeding cup and pins, ca. 1918–1921. (ASCSA Archives, Jack L. Davis Collection)

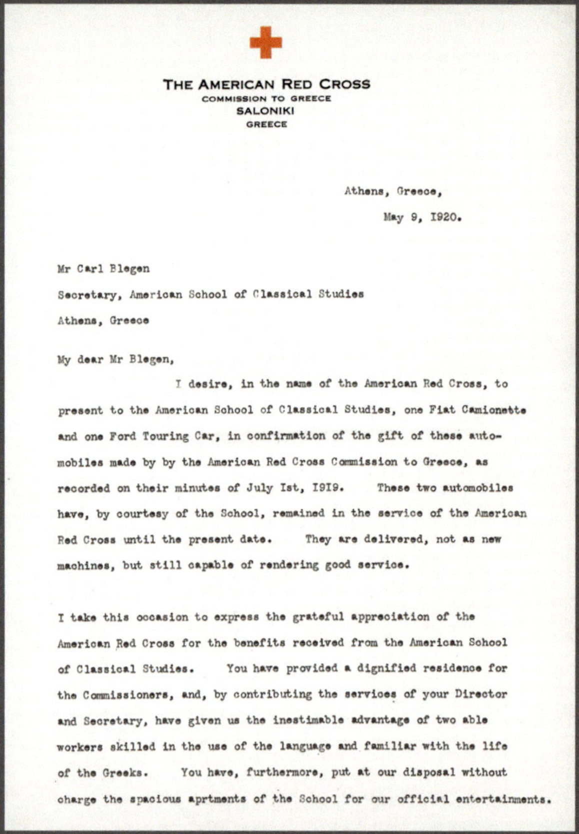

THE AMERICAN RED CROSS
COMMISSION TO GREECE
SALONIKI
GREECE

Athens, Greece,
May 9, 1920.

Mr Carl Blegen
Secretary, American School of Classical Studies
Athens, Greece

My dear Mr Blegen,

I desire, in the name of the American Red Cross, to present to the American School of Classical Studies, one Fiat Camionette and one Ford Touring Car, in confirmation of the gift of these automobiles made by by the American Red Cross Commission to Greece, as recorded on their minutes of July Ist, I9I9. These two automobiles have, by courtesy of the School, remained in the service of the American Red Cross until the present date. They are delivered, not as new machines, but still capable of rendering good service.

I take this occasion to express the grateful appreciation of the American Red Cross for the benefits received from the American School of Classical Studies. You have provided a dignified residence for the Commissioners, and, by contributing the services of your Director and Secretary, have given us the inestimable advantage of two able workers skilled in the use of the language and familiar with the life of the Greeks. You have, furthermore, put at our disposal without charge the spacious aprtments of the School for our official entertainments.

IMPORTANT ITEMS
AMERICAN RED CROSS
SOUTHWESTERN DIVISION
ST. LOUIS, MO.

Vol. II JUNE 3, 1918 No. 22

Nursing Service is Military Service.

The idea of social obligation has taken hold of people during the past few years as never before. Men and women are dedicating themselves to the service of their fellows in increasing numbers. The feeling of noblesse oblige is no longer restricted to a chosen few. It is spreading like a living fire burning up the dry and arid growths of selfishness that obstruct its path. Certain professions have led the way in this humanizing process. Doctors and nurses have ever been ready to spend themselves in behalf of the weak and the suffering. Equipped and trained to serve, they have never failed to respond to the cry of distress. They are responding now, wherever the call has been heard. Many, however, do not yet realize the urgency of the situation. Surgeon General Gorgas has asked for 25,000 Red Cross nurses. Nursing service is Military service, and the trained nurse is as necessary to the successful prosecution of the war as the trained soldier.

Nurses, You Are Needed! Enlist For Service Now!

"Nursing Service is Military Service" featured as a headline in the ARC newsletter of June 3, 1918. (ASCSA Archives, Jack L. Davis Collection)

In 1920 the ARC donated to the American School one Fiat camionette and one Ford Model T touring car as a token of appreciation for the School's good services. "You have provided a dignified residence for the Commissioners, and by contributing the services of your Director and Secretary, have given us the inestimable advantage of two able workers skilled in the use of the language and familiar with the life of the Greek." The School used both cars for its field trips. Donation letter, May 9, 1920. (ASCSA Archives, Carl W. Blegen Papers)

The ARC staff in front of their headquarters at 19 Kephissias Avenue in Athens, 1919. In the front row, third from left, the head of the Greek Commission, Edward Capps. (Khalaf Al Habtoor Archives, Illinois College, Jacksonville, Illinois, Carl E. Black Papers)

Nurse Charlotte M. Heilman (1880–1956) supervised the ARC child welfare stations in Athens. Pictured here, in the middle, with a group of volunteers that she trained. Heilman was the prototype for a character in Ernest Hemingway's *A Farewell to Arms*.(Library of Congress, Prints and Photographs Division, American National Red Cross Photograph Collection)

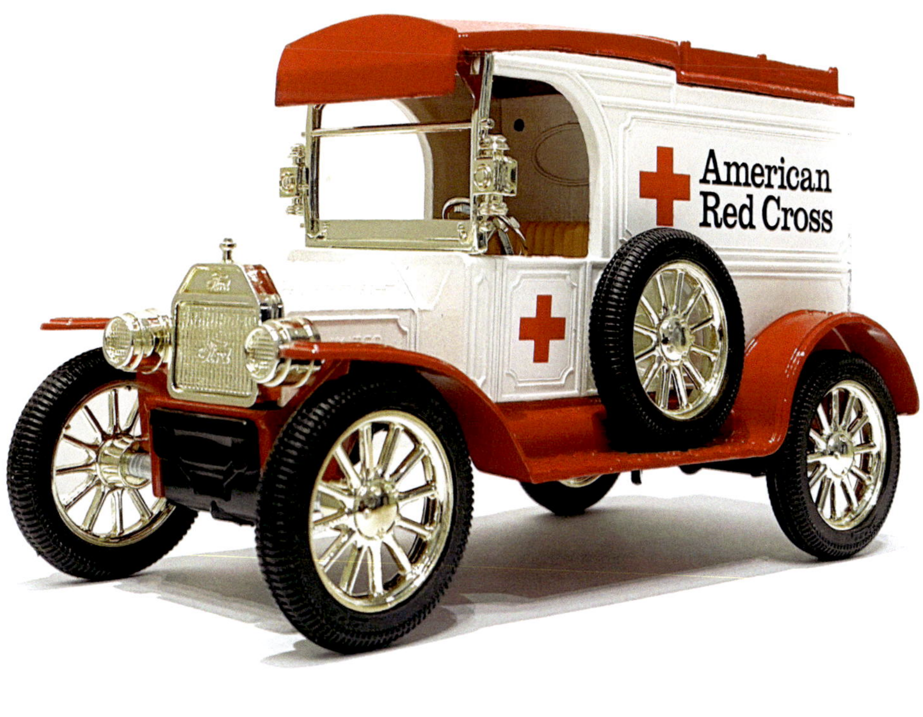

Toy replica of the 1913 Model T used by the ARC in 1919. (ASCSA Archives, Jack L. Davis Collection)

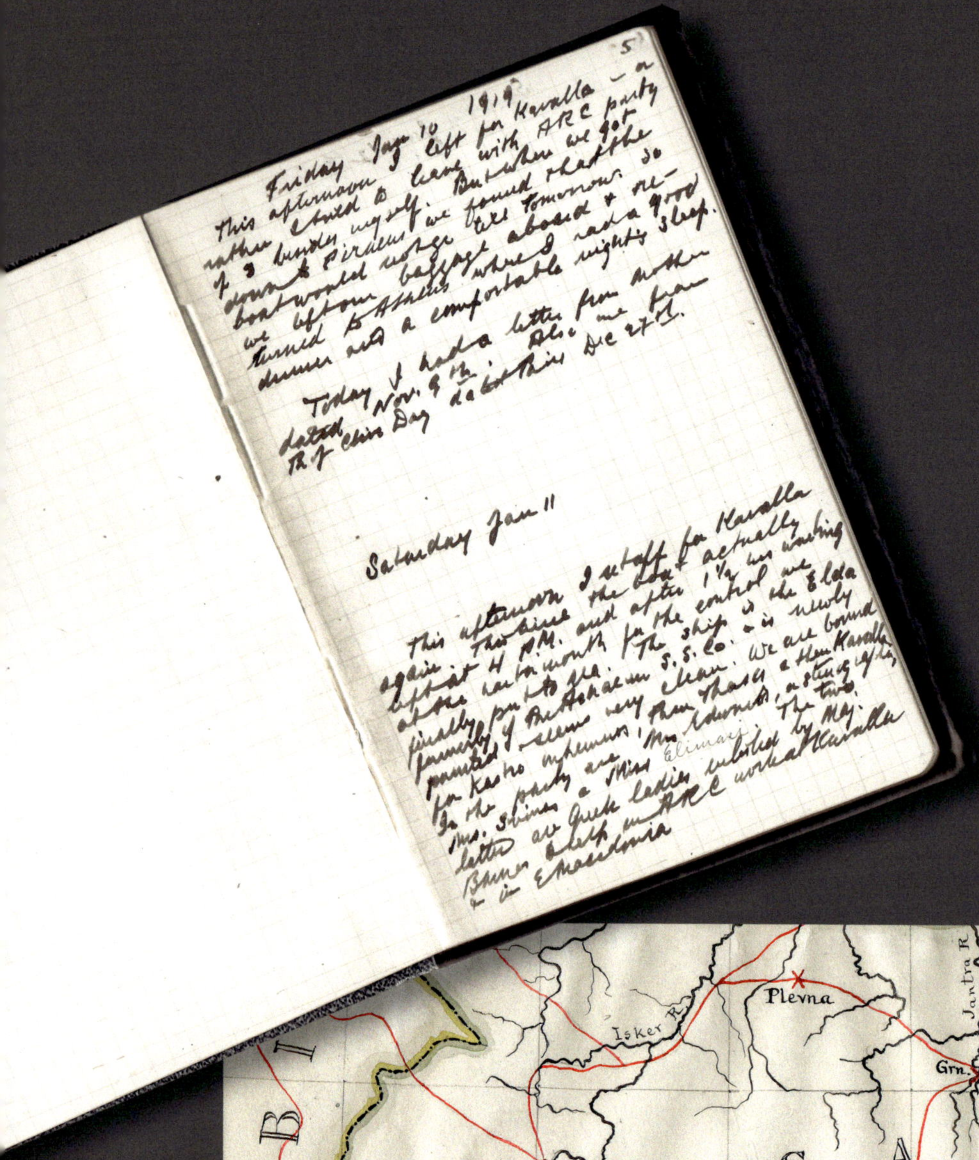

Carl W. Blegen, secretary of the ASCSA (and later a distinguished archaeologist), organized relief efforts in Eastern Macedonia (Mount Pangaion), inspected detention camps in Bulgaria, and delivered medical supplies to Epirus. Here, the diary Blegen kept while in Macedonia and Bulgaria, January 10–May 17, 1919. (ASCSA Archives, Carl W. Blegen Papers)

Hand-drawn map of Eastern Macedonia showing the area of ARC operations and the various relief stations. (Khalaf Al Habtoor Archives, Illinois College, Jacksonville, Illinois, Carl E. Black Papers)

The ARC Headquarters in Kavala, 1919.
"At Kavalla we had no sooner landed than the Americans representing the American tobacco companies offered us a house."
(Horace S. Oakley, *In Macedonia*, Chicago, 1920. ASCSA, Gennadius Library)

ARC soup kitchen at the Zincirli Mosque, Serres, 1919. Major Henry B. Dewing, later first president of Athens College, is visible. (Khalaf Al Habtoor Archives, Illinois College, Jacksonville, Illinois, Carl E. Black Papers)

Distribution warehouse on Chios, 1919. (Newberry Library, Chicago, Horace S. Oakley Papers)

Distribution of clothes, Arachova Street in Athens, 1919. (Library of Congress, Prints and Photographs Division, American National Red Cross Photograph Collection)

Deputy Commissioner and surgeon Carl E. Black (1862–1946) and his team surveyed more than one hundred hospitals, recording their facilities and making recommendations for improvement. Some of the original photos used in Black's *Survey of the Hospitals of Greece* (Athens, 1919) were found in the ASCSA Archives. Photographs of Aiginiteion (above) and Syngros (below) hospitals, 1919. (ASCSA Archives, Archaeological Photographic Collection)

Η ΑΜΕΡΙΚΑΝΙΚΗ ΑΠΟΣΤΟΛΗ ΤΟΥ ΕΡΥΘΡΟΥ ΣΤΑΥΡΟΥ

ΕΙΣ ΤΗΝ ΕΛΛΑΔΑ

ΠΩΣ Η ΕΛΛΑΣ ΜΠΟΡΕΙ ΝΑ ΠΑΡΑΓΗι ΠΕΡΙΣΣΟΤΕΡΗ ΤΡΟΦΗ

ΥΠΟ

ΚΥΡΙΛΛΟΥ ΓΕΩΡ. ΟΠΚΙΝΣ Δ. Φ.

ΤΑΓΜΑΤΑΡΧΟΥ

ΚΑΙ ΥΠΑΡΧΗΓΟΥ ΕΠΙΤΡΟΠΟΥ ΕΝ ΤΗι ΑΜΕΡΙΚΑΝΙΚΗι ΑΠΟΣΤΟΛΗι
ΤΟΥ ΕΡΥΘΡΟΥ ΣΤΑΥΡΟΥ ΕΙΣ ΤΗΝ ΕΛΛΑΔΑ

Ἀποτελέσματα τῆς Ἀσβετόπετρας, Α, καὶ τοῦ Φωσφόρου, Φ, εἰς τὴν καλλειέργιαν τοῦ Μελ λωτου. (Δείγματα ἀπὸ τὸν ἀγρὸν τῶν δοκιμῶν εἰς τὰ Σαγέϊκα. Ἐθερίσθησαν τὴν 28 Ἰουνίου 1919).

Αὔγουστος 1919

ΕΝ ΑΘΗΝΑΙΣ

ΤΥΠΟΙΣ Π. Δ. ΣΑΚΕΛΛΑΡΙΟΥ

1919

The only ARC report published in Greek was that of Major Cyril G. Hopkins (1866–1919), an agricultural chemist, who analyzed more than 3,000 soil samples from all over Greece. His report, *Πως η Ελλάς μπορεί να παράγη περισσότερη τροφή* (*How Greece Can Produce More Food*), recommended the enrichment of Greek soils with calcium, phosphate, and nitrogen. Hopkins contracted typhus and died at Gibraltar in 1919 on his way back to America. (ASCSA, Gennadius Library)

LEST WE PERISH
CAMPAIGN for $30,000,000.
AMERICAN COMMITTEE
FOR RELIEF IN THE NEAR EAST
ARMENIA — GREECE — SYRIA — PERSIA
ONE MADISON AVE., NEW YORK.
CLEVELAND H. DODGE, TREASURER

1B The $30,000,000 Campaign

Opposite: Colored lithograph, 1918. Design by Ethel Franklin Betts for the campaign of the American Committee for Relief in the Near East. (Personal collection of Sharon R. Stocker and Jack L. Davis)

World War I was an unprecedented humanitarian crisis that demanded the assistance of international relief agencies to help with seven million refugees in Europe and Asia Minor.

The persecution of Christian populations in the Ottoman Empire mobilized missionaries and philanthropists to act long before America's entry into the War (1917).

Cleveland H. Dodge, prominent businessman and philanthropist, and James L. Barton, Protestant missionary and educator, created the American Committee for Armenian and Syrian Relief in 1915 to provide emergency humanitarian aid to suffering minority populations in the Ottoman Empire. Chartered by Congress as the Near East Relief (NER) in 1919, the Committee was run initially by one hundred American volunteers whose work targeted the immediate relief and medical assistance of the refugees, and the creation of orphanages and jobs.

World War I was the first major conflict in which all combatant parties made extensive use of propaganda generated by state organs. In April 1917, only a week after the declaration of war on Germany, President Woodrow Wilson established the Committee on Public Information. Its Division of Pictorial Publicity, formed in November of 1917, produced nearly 1,500 designs for propaganda posters, cards, buttons, and cartoons during the war, which were used in the production of films and lantern slides, pamphlets, and magazine advertisements.

In January 1919, the Near East Relief launched a massive $30,000,000 campaign. A dozen renowned artists of the day contributed powerful and iconic designs for the posters that promoted the campaign.

E.D. and J.L.D.

Members of the American Committee for Armenian and Syrian Relief, photographed in 1916. Seated from left: Henry Morgenthau, Cleveland H. Dodge, James L. Barton, and Samuel T. Dutton. Standing from left: Alexander J. Hemphill, Harold A. Hatch, Stanley White, William W. Peet, Edwin M. Bulkley, and Charles V. Vickrey. (James L. Barton, *Story of the Near East Relief*, New York, 1930)

Colored lithograph, 1918. Design by Douglas Volk for the campaign of the American Committee for Relief in the Near East. (Personal collection of Sharon R. Stocker and Jack L. Davis)

Window display with posters for the funds campaign of the American Committee for Armenian and Syrian Relief in Maryland. From *News Bulletin*, published by the American Committee for Armenian and Syrian Relief, April 1919. (Personal collection of Lefteris Zorzos)

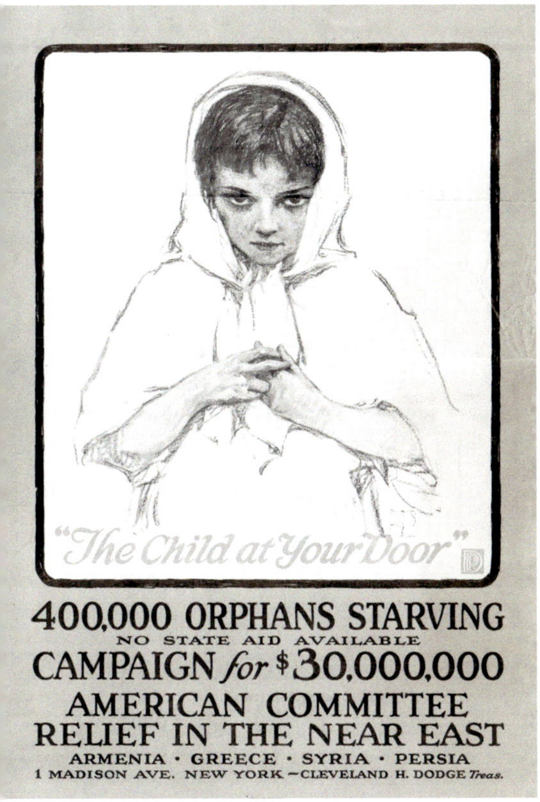

Colored lithograph, 1918. Design by William B. King for the campaign of the American Committee for Relief in the Near East. (ASCSA Archives, Jack L. Davis Collection)

Colored lithograph, 1918. Design by Wladyslaw Theodore Benda for the campaign of the American Committee for Relief in the Near East. (ASCSA Archives, Jack L. Davis Collection)

Colored lithograph, 1918. Design by William B. King for the campaign of the American Committee for Relief in the Near East. (ASCSA Archives, Jack L. Davis Collection)

NEWS BULLETIN

Published by the

American Committee for Armenian and Syrian Relief

One Madison Ave. New York, N.Y.

VOL. III. MAY, 1919 No. 12—Total Number 24

The Newport News before she shed her camouflage.

ANOTHER LIFE BOAT.

The Newport News, fourth transport granted by the United States Navy to the American Committee for Armenian and Syrian Relief, sailed to the rescue of the starving peoples in the Near East April 22nd from New York. The Newport News is bound for Constantinople. She carries five technically trained relief workers to swell the forces already at work in Turkey and a large cargo of clothing and supplies of all kinds for distribution among the destitute millions in that war ravaged land. This is the eighth relief contingent sent out recently by this committee.

Over two hundred persons gathered at Pier 62 of the White Star Line in a farewell service held on the forward deck of the ship before she left on her life saving mission.

Bulletins and informational leaflets contributed to the nationwide fundraising efforts of the American Committee for Armenian and Syrian Relief. The series of bulletins gradually evolved into the monthly magazine *The New Near East*. From *News Bulletin*, published by the American Committee for Armenian and Syrian Relief, May 1919. (ASCSA Archives, Jack L. Davis Collection)

President Wilson appointed Henry Morgenthau (1856–1946) as U.S. ambassador to the Ottoman Empire from 1913 to 1916. Upon his return to the U.S. in 1916, Morgenthau dedicated himself to raising awareness of the plight of the Armenians and the need to help them. In 1923 he headed the Refugee Settlement Commission. (Library of Congress, Prints and Photographs Division, Washington, D.C.)

Issues of the monthly magazine *The New Near East*, January and December 1921. (ASCSA Archives, Joannes Gennadius Papers)

STARVATION
ARMENIA
AND
SYRIA
BRIGGS

REALITIES

TWO and a half million pro-Ally, war stricken Armenian, Syrian, Greek and Persian refugees are absolutely destitute. 400,000 of these who face death from starvation are orphaned children.

The ravages of war and famine have strewn the sands of the deserts and the snows of the mountains with the skeletons of perished victims.

Every $60 means life for one whole year for one refugee.

1c Armenians Fleeing Anatolia

Armenians in the Ottoman Empire faced multiple catastrophes in the early decades of the 20th century. The massacres that began in 1915, now known as the Armenian Genocide, continued well into the 1920s. Surviving and returning Armenians began recovery efforts soon after the Mudros Armistice ended World War I in the Middle Eastern theater in October 1918. Two such efforts were led by the Dildilian family, a family of Armenian photographers who had worked with American missionaries and educators for decades in central and coastal Anatolia. The deprivations and massacres of the war years created thousands of orphans. Aram Dildilian with the aid of his family created an orphanage in Samsun, while his brother Tsolag aided relief efforts in Merzifon on the campus of Anatolia College. These orphanages grew as new waves of violence spread across the region. The Near East Relief (NER) arrived in the region in early 1919.

Following the victory of the Turkish nationalists in the autumn of 1922, the NER was forced to evacuate orphans, staff, and their families to safer spots including Greece. The Dildilians and their charges fled by ship to Piraeus in November 1922. As photographers, they documented their exodus in hundreds of photographs. Sharing these photographs with the NER, they contributed to the humanitarian fundraising efforts by providing visual evidence of the overwhelming needs faced by the organization. Armenians were settled in two refugee camps in the Athens region, one in Kokkinia, near the port of Piraeus, and the other in Dourgouti, inland toward the city center. Tent cities soon became more permanent structures, and churches and schools were built. The Dildilians documented these efforts.

A.T.M.

Opposite: Refugee camp with the Acropolis in the distance, ca. 1923.

Doing laundry at a refugee camp, ca. 1923.

(Dildilian Family Photography Collection)

The first Dildilian photo studio in the Kokkinia camp, ca. 1923.

Refugee family in the Kokkinia camp, ca. 1923.

The first permanent structures built at the refugee camp in Kokkinia on both sides of a stream, ca. 1923.
(Dildilian Family Photography Collection)

The first five orphans rescued by Aram Dildilian with an Armenian priest in front of the Armenian Apostolic Church of Samsun, which served as an orphanage, early 1919.

Armenian and Greek orphans, along with the Dildilians, on the SS *Belgravia* departing Samsun. Mariam Dildilian can be seen in the background on the ladder near the life ring, November 1922.

Refugee camp, ca. 1923.

(Dildilian Family Photography Collection)

Refugees gathering at the Smyrna waterfront as they wait to be evacuated. (Naval History and Heritage Command)

2

THE AMERICAN HUMANITARIAN RESPONSE

Photograph of NER worker and nurse Sara Corning (1872–1969) with orphans evacuated from Smyrna aboard the USS *Litchfield*. Corning helped to evacuate some 5,000 children to Greece. (Yarmouth County Museum and Archives)

The Smyrna Catastrophe

Threatens YOU and All the World —

For the Sake of International Honor, and in Christ's Name, are YOU Doing all You can toward the Establishing of Harmony and the Alleviation of Immediate Suffering?

2A The Smyrna Emergency Relief

The Turkish armed forces under Mustapha Kemal defeated the Greek army in Asia Minor in August 1922. On September 8, the Greek army evacuated Western Asia Minor. A day later, the Turkish army occupied Smyrna. The city was set on fire on September 13, 1922.

On the same day, U.S. President Warren Harding received an appeal to protect the Christian populations. American relief workers from Constantinople and Smyrna rushed to aid the refugees with emergency funds, personnel, and supplies. Five American relief organizations were present in Smyrna: the Near East Relief (NER), the American Red Cross (ARC), the Young Men's Christian Association (YMCA), the Young Women's Christian Association (YWCA), and the American Board of Commissioners for Foreign Missions.

The Turkish authorities had issued the following order: all refugees, except for males of military age, had to depart by September 30 or be deported to the interior. Making provisions for their evacuation was the only way of saving them. By the end of the first week of October, women, children, and the elderly had evacuated Smyrna, under the supervision of the U.S. Navy, the relief organizations, and the assistance of British and Allied naval forces. Hundreds of thousands of refugees managed to secure a safe passage to Greece thanks to the heroic efforts of Asa K. Jennings, the Smyrna YMCA secretary.

A few months later, under the Lausanne Convention (January 30, 1923), Greece and Turkey agreed to the mandatory exchange of populations. Approximately 1.2 million Ottoman Orthodox Christians and 400,000 Greek Muslims were exchanged.

There were also around 150,000 Armenians who found refuge in Greece. Many Armenians saw Greece as a temporary home and left to join families and relatives in other parts of the world, such as the U.S., Europe, Soviet Armenia, and Latin America. A relatively small number, about 64,000 people, remained and settled in Greece.

E.D.

Asa K. Jennings, YMCA field secretary in Smyrna, swiftly organized the evacuation of thousands of refugees to safety in Greece. (Estia Neas Smyrnis)

Asa K. Jennings at Mytilene on the island of Lesvos, a key port of arrival for refugees. (Roger Jennings)

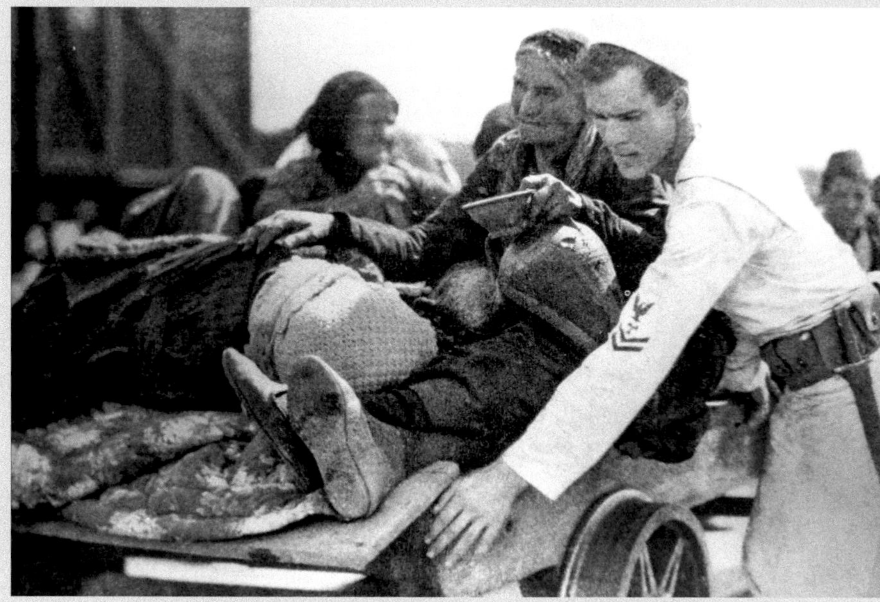

American soldiers assisting refugees to embark on boats. The Greek government awarded the Medal of Military Merit to the commanders of all 12 American destroyers that assisted the refugees.

(*Above: The National Geographic Magazine*, November 1925. Photography C. D. Morris)

(*Left and below:* Booth Family Center for Special Collections, Georgetown University Library, Washington, D.C., George Horton Papers,)

In 1922 George Horton, U.S. Consul in Smyrna, was instrumental in saving Greeks by issuing travel documents that enabled them to evacuate the city. Horton, center, photographed with Maynard Barnes, Vice Consul in Smyrna, and Wallace Treat in early May 1922 visiting the ASCSA excavations at Colophon. (ASCSA Archives, Carl W. Blegen Papers)

Esther Pohl Lovejoy (right, wearing a hat), president of the AWH, was one of the first American relief workers to reach Smyrna. (Esther Pohl Lovejoy, *Certain Samaritans*, New York, 1933. ASCSA, Gennadius Library)

The Smyrna Catastrophe

Threatens YOU and All the World —

The quay of Smyrna after the Catastrophe, with the USS *Edsall* on the left. (Naval History and Heritage Command)

Refugees aboard the USS *Edsall*. The vessel arrived in Smyrna on September 14, 1922, to transfer refugees to Thessaloniki. It returned to Smyrna to continue the rescue operations. (Naval History and Heritage Command)

ng all You
Suffering'

The USS *Scorpion* in the port of Smyrna; it was the flagship of Mark L. Bristol, the U.S. High Commissioner in Constantinople. (Naval History and Heritage Command)

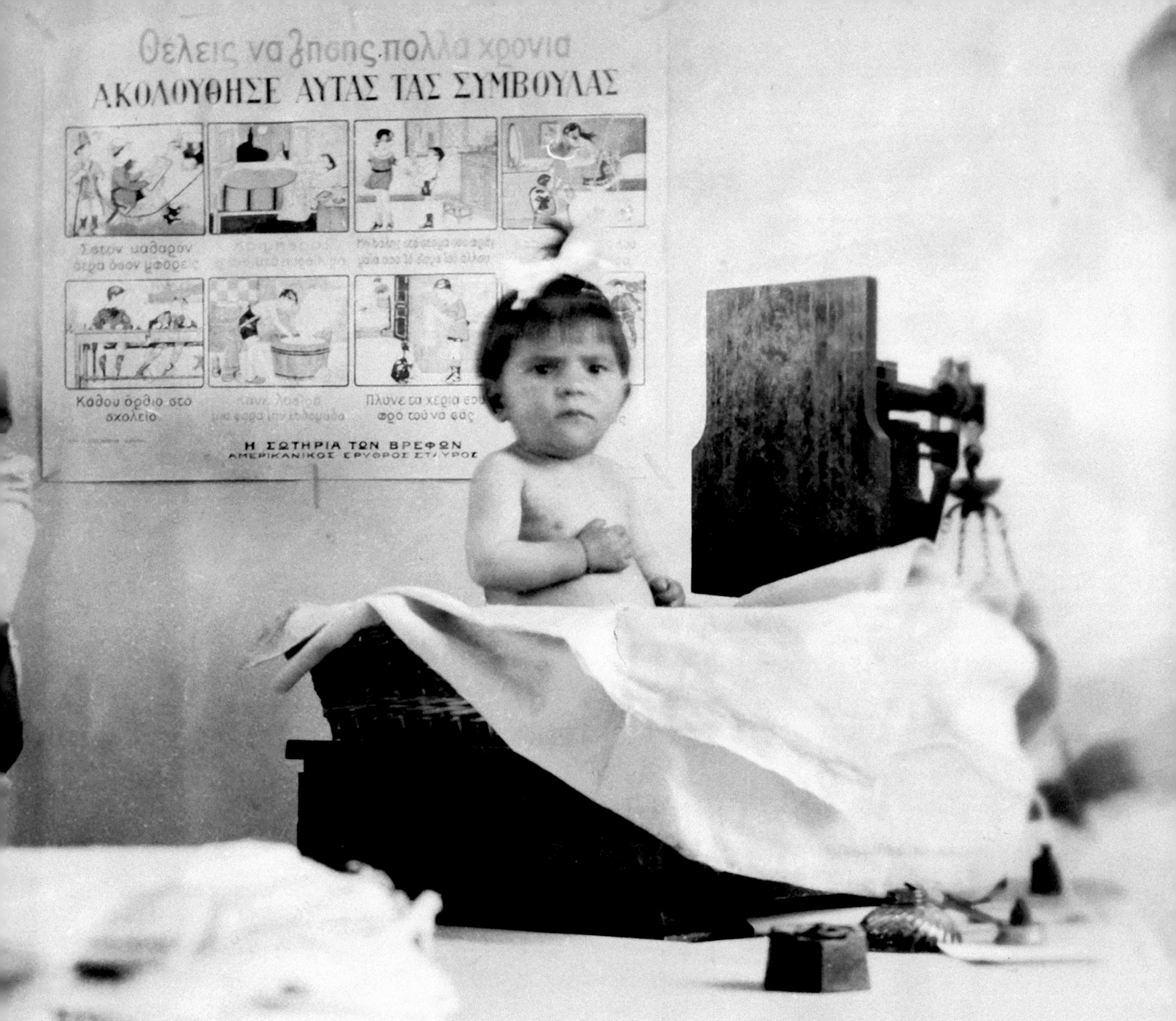

The Red Cross Courier

Official Journal of The American Red Cross

Vol. 3, No. 1. WASHINGTON, D. C., JANUARY 5, 1924 Subscription

SMYRNA REFUGEE SITUATION SOLVED BY ASSIMILATION

American-Athens Relief Committee Reports on Fact To State Department

NEARLY MILLION SAVED

American Red Cross and Greek Government Commended for Solution of Problem

"If you want to live many years, follow this advice." The ARC issued posters with Greek comic strips (like the one seen in the background of this photo) describing best practices for the survival and welfare of infants and children. (Library of Congress, Prints and Photographs Division, American Red Cross Collection)

2B The Return of the American Red Cross to Greece, 1922–1923

Following the Smyrna Disaster, the American community in Athens at the initiative of Darrell O. Hibbard, director of the Young Men's Christian Association (YMCA), and Bert H. Hill, director of the American School of Classical Studies at Athens, joined efforts to seek the support of U.S. humanitarian agencies in assisting the thousands of Asia Minor refugees who had flooded Greece.

By early October, the Athens American Relief Committee (AARC) was formed. Members traveled to many of the Greek islands reporting in detail the refugee situation. Using this report, the Committee was able to raise funding to support one of the first refugee camps, the Lahanagora camp in Piraeus. The AARC was officially dissolved soon after the arrival of the American Red Cross (ARC) but it continued to play a role and produce reports until late in 1923.

The ARC arrived in Greece in October 1922 and stayed until June 1923, spending about $3 million (about $54 million today). During this period the organization sheltered, fed, clothed, and nursed more than 500,000 people, offered services to 58 hospitals, and avoided the spread of epidemics by organizing delousing and bathing plants. On June 24, 1923, King George II of Greece decorated the personnel of the ARC acknowledging their pivotal contribution to the refugee crisis. Believing that it had fulfilled its mission in Greece, the ARC ran press releases with success stories, such as, "Smyrna Refugee Situation Solved by Assimilation."

The premature departure of the ARC was severely criticized. The vacuum left by the departing ARC was filled by a new agency established by the League of Nations in Geneva: the Refugee Settlement Commission, headed by Henry Morgenthau.

N.V.B.

On the evening of June 27, 1923, 37 ARC workers and officials were decorated by the Greek government in an elaborate ceremony. (ERT Archives, Petros Poulides Collection)

The Red Cross Courier

Official Journal of The American Red Cross

Vol. 2. No. 27. WASHINGTON, D. C., JULY 7, 1923 Subscription $1 a Year

AMERICAN RED CROSS COMPLETES ITS EMERGENCY RELIEF OPERATIONS FOR THE SMYRNA REFUGEES

Congestion in Greek Cities

The congestion that prevailed throughout Greece as the result of the influx of nearly a million refugees from Asia Minor is strikingly shown in this picture from Athens.

BROOKLYN, N.Y., CHAPTER AIDS AT RAILWAY WRECK

Sends First Aid Equipment And Squad To Scene Of Fatal Accident

From within a few minutes after the Brooklyn-Manhattan Transit elevated railway wreck at Brooklyn, N. Y., in which eight persons were killed and more than 70 injured, until the night of the third day following the tragedy, Brooklyn's Red Cross Chapter was almost continuously active aiding victims, their families or the police and civil authorities.

As soon as the crash occurred, a First Aid squad was sent to the scene with equipment for helping police and firemen in handling the injured. When the victims had been removed to morgues and hospitials, Home Service workers under the direction of Mrs. Marion Lounsbury Foster, Director, began the arduous task of visiting every family stricken by the death or injury of one of its members.

Every section of Brooklyn, the Borough of Queens and the Borough of Manhattan was covered by these workers in locating families; one worker alone making thirty-five visits.

In this labor the Brooklyn Chapter had the help of the Brooklyn Bureau of Charities, the Queens' Plaza Chapter, the Central Chapter of Queens and the New York County Chapter, each of which cared for several cases within its jurisdiction.

Red Cross Life-Guard Proves Hero in Surf

With thousands of persons lining the boardwalk and pier, the expert Red Cross Life-Saving Corps at Pablo Beach, Fla., added another to its long list of sensational rescues. Ed. Vrieze, of South Jacksonville, a Duval High School student and rated as a surfman in the Red Cross Life-Saving Corps, is acclaimed by Jacksonville papers for the rescue.

Vrieze responded to calls for help from a party of three men and two women who were struggling in a fierce undertow at Pablo Beach. Rushing into the surf with a buoy on his shoulders. Vrieze swam

Dr. Herman Biggs, Of A. R. C. Advisory Committee, Dies

Dr. Herman Michael Biggs, New York State Commissioner of Health, and one of the founders of modern sanitation and preventive medicine, died last week of bronchial pneumonia at his home in New York City. Dr. Biggs was one of the prominent physicians, surgeons and public health officials composing the Red Cross Health Advisory Committee.

Born in Trumansburg, N. Y., he was graduated from Cornell and received his medical degree from Bellevue in 1883. He specialized in bacteriology, then in its infancy. One of his great achievements was the establishment of the bacteriological laboratory in New York City, the first municipal laboratory in the world. Dr. Biggs was appointed a member of the Red Cross Health Advisory Committee in 1922, and subscribed to the report of that Committee early this year unanimously

Italy Has Declined Proffer of Help For Etna Victims

Upon the receipt of news of the recent terrific eruption of Mt. Etna in Sicily the American Red Cross sent through the State Department a cablegram to Ambassador Child at Rome requesting him to express its sympathy to the afflicted people and proffering whatever assistance the organization could give.

Ambassador Child took this offer to the Italian government, and under date of June 26 cabled the following reply:

"Foreign Office expresses warmest thanks to us for proffered assistance, but for the relief work does not need outside help."

---

tenor, concluded the impressive program with a series of songs. Miss Elsie Graves Benedict, European Director of the American Junior Red Cross, headed the Red Cross

Thousands Rescued From Horrors Following Turk Victory

REVIEW OF THE WORK

Vice Chairman Describes Biggest Job Since Armistice

By ERNEST P. BICKNELL

Vice Chairman in Charge of Foreign Operations

Last Saturday, June 30, marked the close of the extensive work which the American Red Cross has been conducting for the refugees who fled into Greek territory from Asia Minor, following the defeat of the Greek army in Turkey and the destruction of Smyrna in September, 1922.

Representatives of the Red Cross reached Smyrna before its capture by the Turks and before its destruction by fire, and did what was possible in cooperation with other agencies to protect and help the refugees during the frightful days of destruction and panic. American ships and sailors and American Red Cross representatives assisted thousands to escape to the hospitable shores of Greece.

BEGINNING OF THE WORK

The large work of the Red Cross, however, began with the assumption by this organization of the burden of caring for the refugees who crowded the ports of both mainland and islands, helpless, destitute, sick, and in general deprived of the support of the men, who had been held as prisoners in Turkey.

Up to the time when these refugees landed in Greece, the Red Cross had been represented by personnel hurried to Smyrna by our Chapter in Constantinople. As soon as the extent of the disaster became known, National Headquarters organized a relief unit under the direction of Dr. A. Ross Hill, at that time Vice Chairman and Director of Foreign

The vice chairman of the ARC described the relief operations in Greece as the "biggest job since the Armistice" in *The Red Cross Courier*, July 7, 1923. (ASCSA Archives)

Quarters for refugees in the Church of the Acheiropoietos, Thessaloniki, 1922. (Library of Congress, Prints and Photographs Division, American National Red Cross Photograph Collection)

The arrival of ARC food supplies at Piraeus, November 1922. (Library of Congress, Prints and Photographs Division, American National Red Cross Photograph Collection)

Refugee child carrying a Borden's condensed milk tin. The NER had commissioned Greek photographer Elli Sougioultzoglou-Seraidari (Nelly's) for a series of photographs of Asia Minor refugees. (Benaki Museum Photographic Archives, Nelly's Collection)

NER pinback pin "Save the Starving in Bible Lands." (ASCSA Archives, Jack L. Davis Collection)

The American Borden Milk company sponsored the NER milk drive of 1924 by agreeing to match the number of cans donated by the American public. Borden's condensed milk tin, 1920s. (ASCSA Archives, Jack L. Davis Collection)

2c The Near East Relief in Greece, 1922–1929

Following the end of World War I, the Near East Relief (NER) expanded its operations with extensive fundraising campaigns and the recruitment of hundreds of relief workers to be engaged at various relief stations in the Near East. Their work included the feeding and clothing of men, women, and children; maintaining and founding hospitals and orphanages; securing safe homes; and creating industrial workshops to encourage refugee adults, especially women, to become self-supporting.

After the Smyrna Catastrophe, the NER transferred its headquarters from Constantinople to Athens. With the cooperation of the Greek government, which secured immediate housing for the orphans in public and private buildings, the organization evacuated 18,500 Armenian and Greek children to Greece, while another 5,000 were transferred to Syria. In subsequent years, the NER established an outplacement program for the children under its care. Armenian orphans were sent abroad and placed with Armenian communities in countries like Egypt and France, where younger children could be adopted by Armenian families and older children were expected to get married (in the case of girls) or to find apprenticeships and employment (in the case of boys).

Five large orphanages were operating by 1923: in the Zappeion exhibition center and in parts of the Old Palace in Athens, in Oropos, Corfu, Corinth, and on the island of Syros.

The Near East Relief Syros orphanage was the largest; built on a huge piece of land donated by the Greek state, it housed up to 5,000 children. In addition to providing food, shelter, and a comprehensive elementary education, special clinics were run in collaboration with the American Women's Hospitals to treat favus, trachoma, and malaria. Children over 10 years of age were given vocational training in purpose-built workshops. Boys were trained as carpenters, farmers, mechanics, shoemakers, silversmiths, and potters, and the girls as dressmakers, weavers, and nurses.

The Near East Relief ran its orphan-related programs in Greece until 1929, by which time the children under its care had been placed with families, had become self-supporting, or had become of age. After 1930 the organization, under the name Near East Foundation, continued to support initiatives in health care, vocational education, and rural development.

Jackie Coogan, known as "America's Boy," participated in NER's milk campaign. Coogan visited Athens in October 1924. (Paul Farnham and Library Special Collections, Charles E. Young Research Library, UCLA, Adelbert Bartlett Papers)

NER orphans in front of the Pantheon movie theater waiting to watch a Charlie Chaplin movie with Jackie Coogan. (ERT Archives, Petros Poulides Collection)

Cover of *The New Near East* Magazine, May 1921. (ASCSA Archives, Joannes Gennadius Papers)

Hat, jacket sleeve, and embroidered pieces of children's clothing from the NER orphanage on Syros. (The Near East Relief Syros Project)

Orphans on Syros "sing" Christmas greetings, 1925. (Anatolia College Archives and Special Collections)

The "Golden Rule Sunday" campaign initiated by the NER's general secretary, Charles V. Vickrey, was launched across the U.S. on Sunday, December 2, 1923. Families were urged to replace their elaborate Sunday meal with a simple meal like those served in NER orphanages and to donate the money they would save. NER sign for the "Golden Rule Sunday" campaign. (ASCSA Archives, Jack L. Davis Collection)

Meals served to the NER orphans. (https://neareastmuseum.com/2015/05/29/fighting-hunger/)

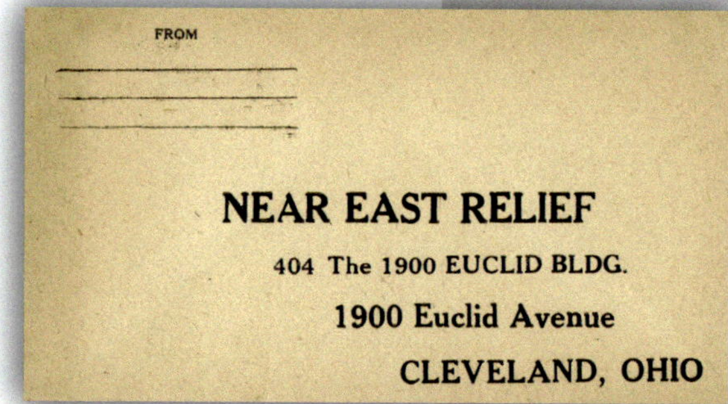

Envelope with the NER address, ca. 1920s. (ASCSA Archives, Jack L. Davis Collection)

NER Zappeion orphans photographed in front of the Temple of Zeus in Athens while receiving health care services. (ERT Archives, Petros Poulides Collection)

Left: Dorothy H. Sutton, ca. 1920. (ASCSA Archives, Dorothy H. Sutton Papers)

Right: Alice G. Carr, ca. 1917–1919. (Wright State University Libraries, Special Collections and Archives)

The personal testimonies and stories of the Near East Relief workers reflect the selflessness and empathy of American humanitarian relief.

DOROTHY H. SUTTON (1878–1970) joined the Near East Relief (NER) overseas personnel and worked in Constantinople, Erivan, Ismit, and Greece between 1920 and 1926. At the end of 1922 she escorted 900 orphan girls from Constantinople to Loutraki, where she was put in charge of the NER orphanage. She followed the children to the island of Cephalonia, where she served as director of the Cephalonia orphanage and subsequently served for a short time at the Syros orphanage. Before returning to the U.S., she ran the NER Thessaloniki Child Welfare Department until its closure in April 1926.

ALICE G. CARR (1887–1968) served in Europe as an ARC nurse during World War I and was subsequently posted to Arta as chief of the Unit of Epirus in 1923 to fight smallpox and typhus among the refugees. In April 1923 and for the next 22 years, she joined the Near East Relief rising to the post of the Director of Public Health in Greece. She dedicated her life to the fight against typhus, malaria, and tuberculosis; she also established child welfare centers and health clinics, with an emphasis on hygiene. At the NER Syros orphanage, she oversaw the health department and the Nurses Training School. Later, at the NER Corinth orphanage, she managed to control a terrible outbreak of malaria thanks to the assistance of the Greek government, the local authorities, and a group of the NER orphan boys.

E.D.

The NER organized nationwide appeals for donations of secondhand clothing, under the name "Bundle Days." Photograph of refugee women employed by the NER in Thessaloniki to sort and repair used clothing from America. (James L. Barton, *Story of the Near East Relief*, New York, 1930)

The pharmacy and the headquarters of the AWH in Athens, at 9 Academias Street. (Legacy Center Archives, Drexel University College of Medicine, American Women's Hospitals Records)

2D American Women's Hospitals in Greece

The organization American Women's Hospitals (AWH) was created in 1917 to encourage the participation of American women physicians in the war effort and push for the advancement of women in the medical profession. Dr. Esther Lovejoy served as the first president of the organization (1919–1967). By November 1919, over 1,000 female physicians had registered to offer their services. After the end of the war most of them remained in the field in France, Serbia, and the Near East to provide medical assistance and establish health programs.

The AWH responded immediately to the needs of refugees from Asia Minor and assumed responsibility for providing full medical care to the Near East Relief orphans transferred to Greece. The women doctors and nurses of the AWH devoted themselves to treating typhus, malaria, trachoma, dengue fever, and tuberculosis. They operated hospitals in Athens and the islands: a 75-bed hospital in Piraeus, a 25-bed hospital in Kokkinia, a 40-bed hospital at the Phaleron airport, and hospitals on various islands (Crete, Lesvos, Chios). In addition, the organization administered clinics inside the Near East Relief orphanages in Greece, baby stations in cities and refugee camps, and traveling automobile clinics.

The American Women's Hospitals continued to operate hospitals, clinics, and health centers in Greece beyond 1929. In the words of Apostolos Doxiadis, the Greek Minister of Relief: "Greece owes a debt of gratitude to the American Women's Hospitals which crossed the ocean to put the spirit of method and organization as well as the generous heart of the American women at the service of more than a million distressed refugees."

E.D.

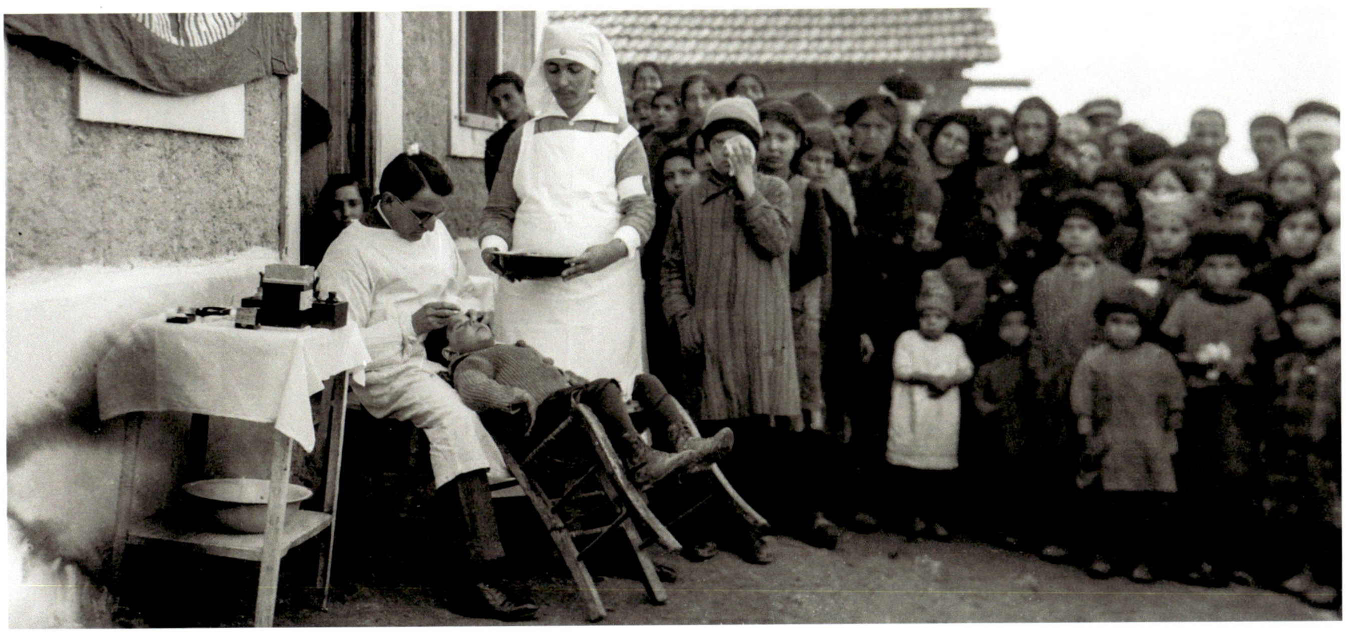

Dr. Ananias Gavriilides, the head of the Dourgouti Eye Clinic at the AWH, and nurses treating children suffering from trachoma. (Legacy Center Archives, Drexel University College of Medicine, American Women's Hospitals Records)

Children receiving trachoma treatment at the Dourgouti Eye Clinic. Trachoma, an infectious eye disease, was common among refugees and children in NER orphanages.

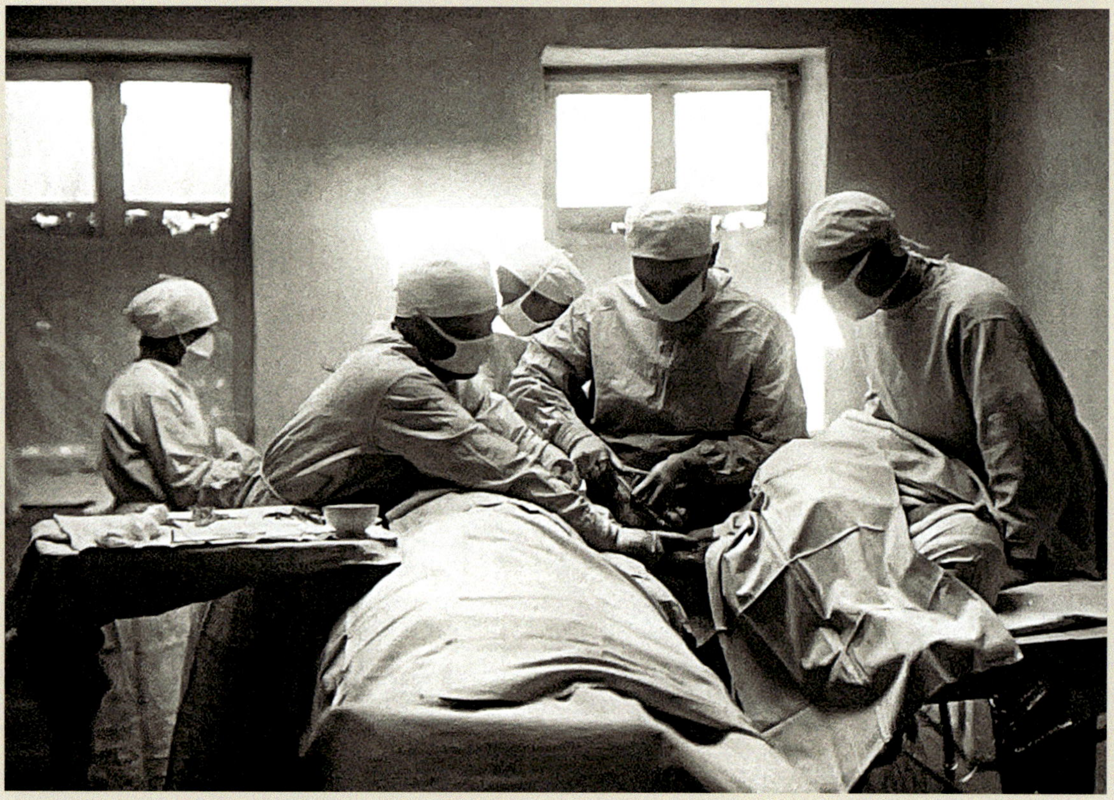

View of the operating room of the American Women's Hospitals at Kokkinia. The AWH provided out-patient services while operating clinics, a hospital, and a nursing school.

(Legacy Center Archives, Drexel University College of Medicine, American Women's Hospitals Records)

A little inhabitant of Macronisos carrying water for his family in one of the camps.

One of the seven camps on Macronisos quarantine station that functioned from February to June 1923 under the supervision of the AWH.

(Legacy Center Archives, Drexel University College of Medicine, American Women's Hospitals Records)

Olga Stastny with a group of Macronisos's little inhabitants. Before Macronisos, Stastny had run several projects on behalf of the AWH in Prague (a child welfare program, a training program for nurses, and a campaign against tuberculosis). (Esther Pohl Lovejoy, *Certain Samaritans*, New York, 1933. ASCSA, Gennadius Library)

OLGA STASTNY (1878–1952), graduate of the University of Nebraska Medical School, was, in 1923, the director of the AWH quarantine station on Macronisos Island off the coast of Attica. Eight thousand people were transferred to the island because they had been exposed to typhus and smallpox. The organization provided food for the refugees with the assistance of the American Red Cross. Water, fuel, and transportation were covered by the Greek state. For her courage Stastny was awarded the Silver Cross of the Order of the Savior by King George II.

Quinine is the principal alkaloid extracted from the dried bark of the tropical cinchona tree. It was used to treat many diseases, especially malaria. (Museum of Pharmacology, Medical School of Athens)

Ruth Parmelee (top row, center) with a group of graduating student nurses in front of the Greek and American flags. One of the greatest legacies of the AWH was the nursing school they maintained in Kokkinia, which trained hundreds of nurses. (Legacy Center Archives, Drexel University College of Medicine, American Women's Hospitals Records)

RUTH AZNIV PARMELEE (1885–1973) was born in Turkey to missionary parents and received her medical degree from the University of Illinois. Under the American Board of Commissioners for Foreign Missions she offered her medical services to the Harpoot region, where she also trained nurses and cared for 3,000 orphans of the war. In October 1922, she established and directed the AWH Thessaloniki, assisted by a group of refugee physicians and nurses. From 1925 to 1933 Parmelee was medical director of the AWH at Kokkinia. In 1924 she was decorated with the Silver Cross of the Order of the Savior by King George II.

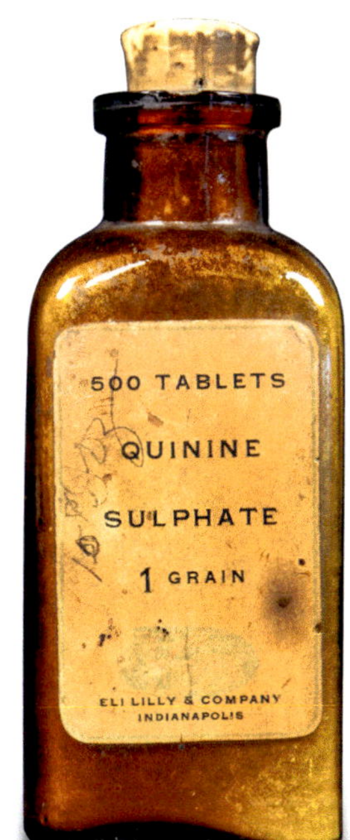

Glass container for quinine tablets, Eli Lilly and Company, ca. 1920s. (ASCSA Archives, Jack L. Davis Collection)

From 1924 to 1930, the salesrooms of the AFG Workshops were housed together with the offices of the NER, at 48 Amalias Avenue, opposite the Arch of Hadrian. (Rockefeller Archive Center, Near East Foundation Records)

3

RENDERING THE REFUGEES SELF-SUFFICIENT

"Won't you look into the workshop with me? The room, about twenty feet square, has no furnishings except benches. Forty women and girls are there, from eleven years up to any age where the woman has eyes to see. They are embroidering little Greek bags with designs taken from the old pottery of Rhodes. […] The silk we use here is taken from cocoons grown near Kalamata. […] We have the raw silk dyed just the shade to match the beautiful colors in Rhodian pots and antique scarfs. When the bags and dresses and scarfs are finished they are sent to America," wrote Gladys Slade Thompson in *American Workshops in Greece: A 1924 Experiment Becomes a 1925 Fact*, Washington, D.C., 1925.

3A Edward Capps and the American Friends of Greece

Following the withdrawal of the American Red Cross (ARC) in June 1923, many Americans with firsthand knowledge of the situation in Greece felt that the refugees were still facing death from slow starvation. Initiated and chaired by Edward Capps, chair of the Managing Committee of the American School of Classical Studies at Athens, the American Friends of Greece (AFG) was incorporated on October 16, 1923. The organization's membership list included many important American philhellenes associated with academia, businesses, and philanthropic foundations.

Non-sectarian and non-political, the organization aimed at acquainting the American people with the real facts in Greece, including the reluctance of the U.S. government to pay to Greece the balance of the Tripartite Loan of 1918; at cooperating with existing charitable organizations willing to undertake relief work in Greece; and at launching new appeals for funds.

In a series of press releases issued in the early months of 1924, the AFG countered announcements from the ARC that the Greek refugee problem had been solved. Under pressure from the AFG and other U.S. relief organizations, the ARC finally agreed to ship five tons of quinine to Greece without, however, resuming a new program of relief aid.

Disappointed with the results of its efforts to convince the U.S. government that Greece was still in need, the AFG dropped its general appeal for relief aid, concentrating solely on the development of embroidery workshops, the products of which would be sold in America, creating income for the refugees.

The AFG embroidery workshops operated as such for about two years, with W. Stuart Thompson (architect of the Gennadius Library) and his wife Gladys acting as Athens representatives. In 1926 Priscilla Capps, daughter of Edward, took over the management of the workshops.

N.V.B.

In 1927 Koula Simernitsa or Simernitski bought an American Singer sewing machine. The privileged owner of one could contribute to the family income by accepting commissions from workshops like those of NEI. In 1940 Koula sold her Singer to Elisavet Koukoutou, who years later said, "it saved us during the German Occupation because it allowed us to dress ourselves if we could secure some fabric. [...] I have even sewn sheets and curtains with it." (Personal collection of Elisavet Komninou)

E.C. 5 Jan '24

AMERICAN FRIENDS OF GREECE, INC.

FOR AID TO GREECE AND THE REFUGEES OF THE NEAR EAST

THE CRITICAL SITUATION

The outstanding event in the Near East with which the world must reckon is the triumph of Turkish "nationalism." The Christian minorities of Turkey are no longer on Turkish soil. The last vestige of Greek culture and civilization has been swept from Asia Minor.

There is no need to tell again the story of the flight of the terror-stricken Christians from lands their ancestors had tilled for countless generations; less need to recount the horror of the sack and burning of Smyrna. These events, unparallelled since the dark ages, are still fresh in the minds of all, but few realize that after the first short, sharp terror of flight, when massacre, robbery, torture, rape and all varieties of agony mingled in utter confusion, the present situation of hundreds of thousands of human beings is even worse than in those days when instant death stared them in the face. *Today the refugees are again face to face with death—death from slow starvation.*

During those dark days of the autumn of 1922, it was the American Navy and the American relief organizations that helped and directed the flight of the refugees to Greece, and the refugees were taken to Greece, not because they had a legal claim to asylum there, but because no other country in the world would receive them.

It is not necessary to refer to the work of the American Red Cross in Greece and the Near East Relief in Asia Minor during the winter of 1922–3—that story is well known and has been repeatedly told to the American people. Today, however, *no American organization is contributing to the support of the great mass of refugees in Greece*—the Near East Relief is doing splendid work with the orphans which it brought to Greece from Asia Minor (two-thirds of them Armenians) and the American Women's Hospitals is doing equally fine work in its own sphere of action, but aside from this *so far as America is concerned the refugees have been deserted.*

When the American Red Cross decided in March, 1923, that it would withdraw from Greece in June, it seems to have considered its decision justified by the approach of summer, the prospect of good crops, and the hope that the renewal of the Lausanne Conference would bring speedy peace and some definite solution of the whole problem. Unfortunately these hopes were not realized. Summer came it is true, and for a while alleviated the suffering of the refugees, but the crops were poor, and even if they had been good they could not have met the needs of a population increased by more than twenty-five per cent.

The Lausanne conference dragged on interminably, due to no fault of Greece, but to the wrangling between Turkey and the Western Powers over oil, concessions and capitulations.

While this was going on Greece had to keep an army on the frontier to maintain its territorial integrity. The Italian seizure of Corfu shortly after the close of the Lausanne conference again made demobilization impossible. The indemnity unjustly handed over to Italy by the Council of Ambassadors was a sum almost equal to the entire expenditure of the American Red Cross in Greece. *Mussolini at a single stroke thus completely nullified the financial aid given to Greece by America's greatest relief organization.*

In a press release on December 1, 1923, the AFG explained to the American public why the money raised by the Refugee Settlement Commission could not be used for temporary relief and announced that there were still 300,000 destitute people who needed support. "The question to be considered is not Can America afford to help, but Can America afford not to help?" (ASCSA Archives, Bert H. Hill Papers)

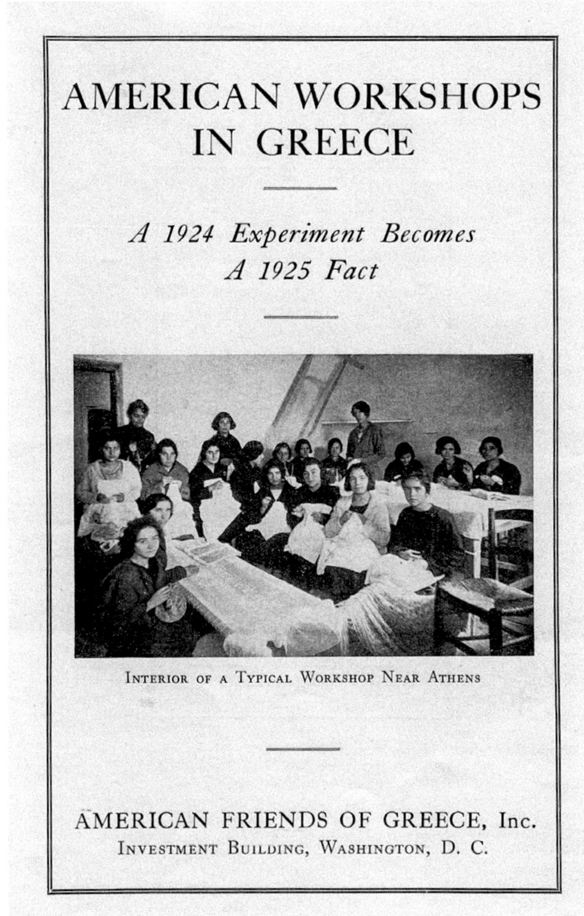

AMERICAN WORKSHOPS IN GREECE

A 1924 Experiment Becomes A 1925 Fact

Interior of a Typical Workshop Near Athens

AMERICAN FRIENDS OF GREECE, Inc.
Investment Building, Washington, D. C.

To support the women refugees in a constructive way, the AFG directed its efforts at establishing embroidery workshops. The AFG ran two such workshops, one in the Koundouriotis camp (below) built by Greek-Americans, the other in Pangrati built by the Refugee Settlement Commission. (Gladys Slade Thompson, *American Workshops in Greece: A 1924 Experiment Becomes a 1925 Fact*, Washington, D.C., 1925)

Gilbert C. Scoggin, first librarian of the Gennadius Library; his wife Susan; and Grace and Edward Capps, outside the newly built library, ca. 1926. Note the string handbag that Mrs. Scoggin is holding. (ERT Archives, Petros Poulides Collection)

W. Stuart Thompson, the architect of the Gennadius Library, and his wife Gladys Slade Thompson, ca.1928. (ASCSA Archives)

String handbag attributed to the AFG Workshops. (ASCSA Archives, April D. Michas Collection)

A brochure advertising the embroideries of the AFG Workshops before Priscilla Capps took over, most likely made before AFG came under the aegis of the NER, ca. 1925–1926. (University of Washington Libraries, Special Collections)

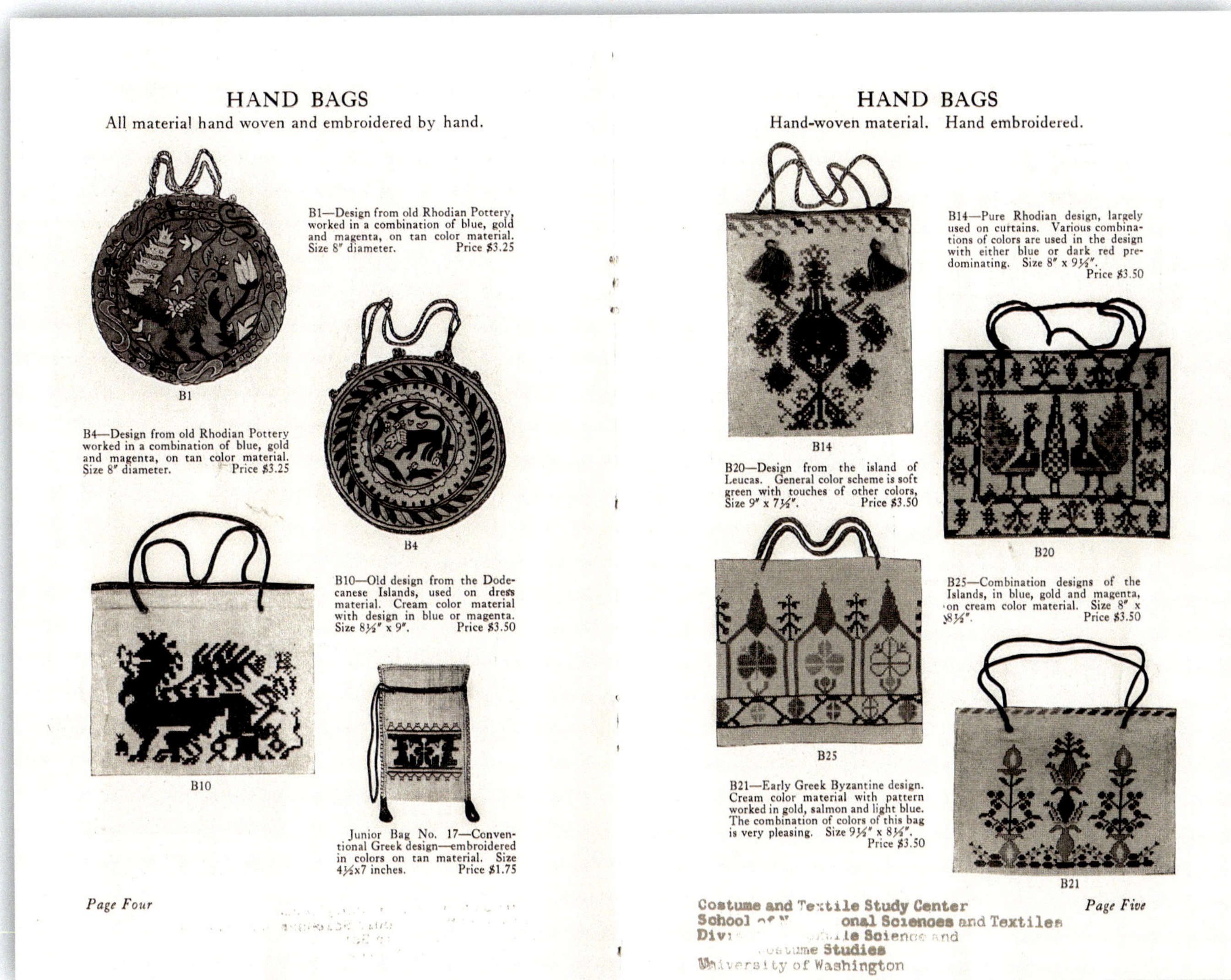

HAND BAGS

All material hand woven and embroidered by hand.

B1—Design from old Rhodian Pottery, worked in a combination of blue, gold and magenta, on tan color material. Size 8″ diameter. Price $3.25

B1

B4—Design from old Rhodian Pottery worked in a combination of blue, gold and magenta, on tan color material. Size 8″ diameter. Price $3.25

B4

B10—Old design from the Dodecanese Islands, used on dress material. Cream color material with design in blue or magenta. Size 8½″ x 9″. Price $3.50

B10

Junior Bag No. 17—Conventional Greek design—embroidered in colors on tan material. Size 4½x7 inches. Price $1.75

Page Four

HAND BAGS

Hand-woven material. Hand embroidered.

B14—Pure Rhodian design, largely used on curtains. Various combinations of colors are used in the design with either blue or dark red predominating. Size 8″ x 9½″. Price $3.50

B14

B20—Design from the island of Leucas. General color scheme is soft green with touches of other colors, Size 9″ x 7½″. Price $3.50

B20

B25—Combination designs of the Islands, in blue, gold and magenta, on cream color material. Size 8″ x 8½″. Price $3.50

B25

B21—Early Greek Byzantine design. Cream color material with pattern worked in gold, salmon and light blue. The combination of colors of this bag is very pleasing. Size 9½″ x 8½″. Price $3.50

B21

Page Five

Priscilla Capps clad in Skyrian bridal costume, 1925. In 1972 Priscilla Capps and her husband Harry Hill donated her embroidery collection, including this Skyrian costume, to the Museum of Fine Arts, Boston. (ASCSA Archives, Oscar Broneer Papers)

3B Priscilla Capps and the Near East Industries

Incorporation of the American Friends of Greece (AFG) in 1923 marked the start of Priscilla Capps's involvement in refugee affairs. Priscilla (1900–1985), a graduate of Smith College, had assisted her father Edward Capps in Athens during his service as U.S. Minister to Greece (1920–1921). Priscilla's hereditary deafness did not prevent her from being active and entrepreneurial.

In 1926 Priscilla undertook the management of the AFG Workshops. By 1928, the AFG Workshops were consolidated with the Near East Relief Industrial Department, rebranding themselves as Near East Industries (NEI). After 1931 the NEI in Greece operated under the aegis of the Near East Foundation.

Priscilla had a deep knowledge of Greek folk art, herself owning a collection of regional embroideries and costumes, such as the one from Skyros (today in the Museum of Fine Arts, Boston).

In Athens the NEI products were first available for purchase in Priscilla's shop at 48 Amalias Avenue, across from the Arch of Hadrian, and, after 1931, at 2 Amalias Avenue, near Syntagma Square. They were also sold on cruise ships. At first the production was limited to embroidered bags, purses, luncheon sets, suits, and dresses. The production of small dolls clad in traditional garments by the Near East Industries in Greece did not start until 1932. In addition to Priscilla's enterprise in Athens, the Near East Foundation also produced dolls in Sofia, Bulgaria.

J.L.D and N.V.B.

Small purse in cross-stitch, a string bag made of pieces of fabric combined in a pattern, and a small string bag featuring a horse, a popular theme for the NEI, copied from Greek Geometric art. (ASCSA Archives, Jack L. Davis and April D. Michas Collections)

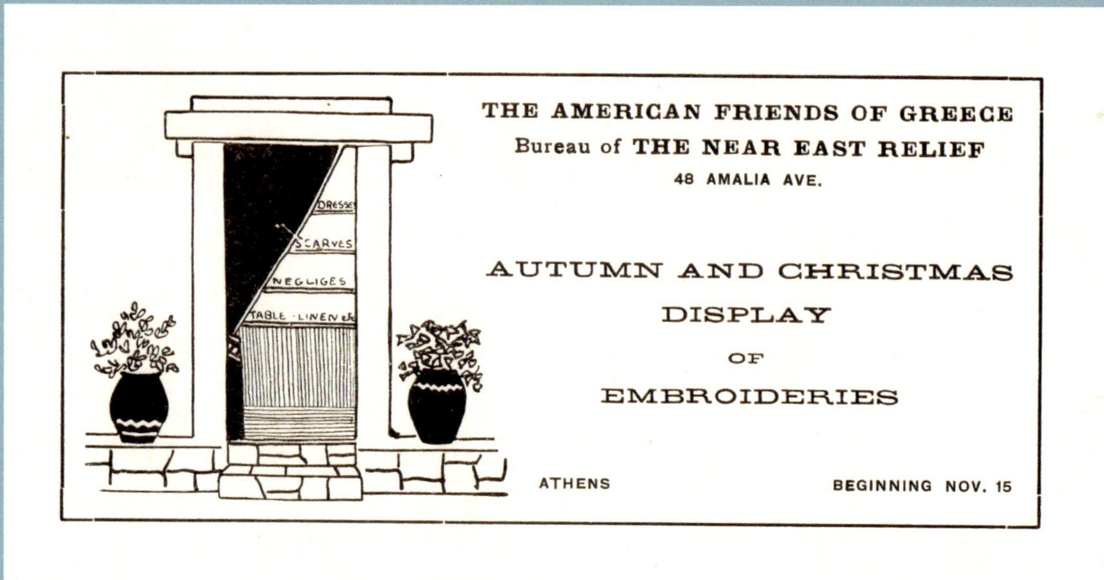

Card advertising the embroideries produced by the AFG Workshops, under the aegis of the NER, ca. 1926–1930. (ASCSA Archives, Mary Zelia Pease Philippides Papers)

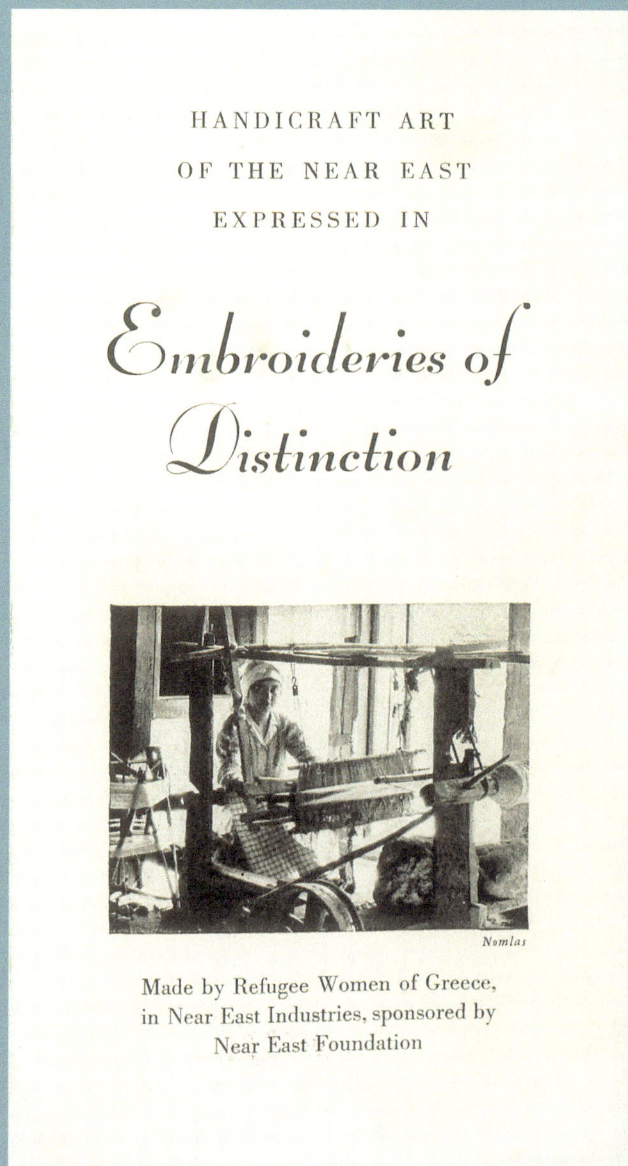

Left: A full-page advertisement in Brainerd P. Salmon's *Glimpses of Greece* (Washington, D.C., 1928) showing a view through the Arch of Hadrian to the NER offices at 48 Amalias Avenue, which also housed the salesrooms of the AFG Workshops in Athens. *Right:* Leaflet advertising NEI products.

Leaflet advertising the products of the NEI in Athens (with map location inside), ca. 1932. (ASCSA Archives, Jack L. Davis Collection)

Handmade tablecloth made of *cocolarico* (raw silk cloth made of salvaged broken cocoons). *Cocolarico* was advertised as a miraculous product that looked like fine linen but "it does not wrinkle, crush or lose its shape even through the roughest usage." Produced by the AFG Workshops, ca. 1926–1929. (ASCSA Archives, April D. Michas Collection)

8 THE ENQUIRER, CINCINNATI, TUESDAY, OCTOBER 10, 1933

IN SOCIETY

"THE GLORY THAT WAS GREECE"

YESTERDAY the intelligentzia of his region was intrigued to learn that late this month there will appear upon the newsstands and in discriminating homes of this vicinity, a monthly magazine which is to be known as The Cincinnati Spectator. Its promoters, clever and experienced though they be, lay no claim to the genius that gave the immortal Addison and Steele so great an influence upon their time, as the inspiration of the famous Eighteenth Century "London Spectator." They do hope, however, to give to the Queen City of the West and its neighbors a magazine dedicated to society and civic matters that will rival such publications as The Spur, The New Yorker, The Chicagoan and similar publications already successfully conducted.

A staff of energetic writers enrolled both at home and abroad, some of them nationally famous, will contribute to these pages illuminating and entertaining comment in the realm of the theater, books, society clubs, music, the home, gardening, sports, fashions, letters, politics, finance, travel, the radio, antiques, interior decorating, personalities, humor, photography, education, literature, poetry, art and current events.

The publishers of the Cincinnati Spectator, working separately on this idea for some six years, came together by chance and pooled their information and ideals. They propose to ride the tide of optimism now sweeping the country and to create something worthwhile and constructive that shall be a credit to a community which, through its record in times of stress, has earned a national reputation for courage and conservatism.

It is this "quixotic adventure," as Mr. O. O. McIntyre has called it, that will soon intrigue and, it is anticipated, inform and amuse a city known for its culture and respected for its appreciation.

The personnel dominating this undertaking includes Messrs. Everett M. Boyd as Editor; Lee E. Davis, Managing Editor; John Moore, Literary Editor; W. E. Mackelfresh Jr., Art Director; Donald G. Boyd, Business Manager; Thomas Price, Advertising Manager; Daniel Farny, assistant to Mr. Price.

In addition to these principals, a group of prominent Cincinnatians, men and women, will be invited to serve on an editorial board in an advisory capacity to help shape the Spectator's policy and lend new dignity to a timely and advantageous project.

In the forthcoming November issue of Cincinnati's swankiest magazine there will be contributions by Messrs. Walter E. Siple, J. H. Thuman, Frank Aston, Charlton Wallace, William Galt, A. R. Theobald, Harry Pence, Charles H. Purdy, William E. Minor, Miss Marion Devereux and others.

Thus will be launched an undertaking which promises to give hostages to dullness and offer incentive to congratulation.

TOWN CLUB ACTIVITIES.

With the return of society from Spa and summer villa and the autumn shopping which brings Dame Fashion from country and suburban life to take a look at the shops, the Town Club teems with interest.

Intriguing remodeling goes on in the big dining room on the Fourth and Vine Street corner, this spacious retreat being now redecorated under the aegis of the board and with the expert advice of Mr. Urban Morgan, just home from an inspiring summer in Europe.

Mr. George Lathrop Williams, the President, has made various recent appointments which give new eclat to this smart organization atop the Sinton-St. Nicholas.

Mrs. Horace Schmidlapp has accepted the Chairmanship of this winter's symphony teas, to the great delight of her fellow members. None better than she can perpetuate the hospitable traditions established last year by her predecessor, Mrs. Albert James Bell.

Mrs. Schmidlapp is now preparing a plan of procedure with her customary discrimination, these arrangements being still in a state of flux but with tremendously interesting prospects.

As the symphony concerts have this year been reduced to 16 instead of following the precedent set last winter, these symphony teas in honor of Mr. and Mrs. Goossens and the soloists brought here for these impressive musical events, take on a special social and artistic significance.

Mrs. Albert James Bell, who is recovering remarkably well from her recent serious illness, has taken over the chairmanship of hospitality.

In that connection she has asked Mrs. John Crawford Pogue to take charge of a series of dances, the dates for which have not yet been chosen. There will be two or three of these, which gives opportunity to make each informal and attractive.

The famous exchange of populations following the World War, involving a return of the Greeks to their native soil from Asia Minor, is one of the epics of modern times. It brought about a special providence in the shape of the Near East Industries, which, in Athens, under the directorship of Miss Pricilla Capps, has made refugee families with dependent children self-supporting, and which has restored, and interpreted in various beautiful and useful ways, "the glory that was Greece." For, in establishing these refugees in a school of handicraft, the Near East Industries have revived the deathless arts for which the fleet fingers of their ancestors through 2,000 years have been famous.

Today and tomorrow, at the residence of Mr. and Mrs. William Tunstall Semple on Pike Street, Miss Capps's display of articles fashioned after designs that are historic in their significance and marvelous in their execution and color will give the seeker after the sort of handwork which is authentic and rare a thrill second to none.

No. 1 in the above photograph is one of the spiffiest of the dolls done in peasant costume that fringe the bookshelves of Mr. and Mrs. Semple's library. Somewhere in Cincinnati there is a child or a collector for each one of these jaunty, gay-gowned figures. The one here shown is particularly characteristic, all "dolled up" to perfection from striped wool socks to flowing headgear. All these figurines are similar to those made especially by the Near East Industries for their exhibit at A Century of Progress in Chicago.

No. 2, is a reproduction of a classic theme, made into a long slender runner, very usable, smart and lovely. The horse figures often in Greek art of this period, and is here presented in its symbolic guise. Miss Capps shows this design in different bright or pale tones done on the soft raw silk that never creases and apparently wears forever even in the face of the most recalcitrant laundry or the roughest handling.

No. 3 suggests to the Christmas shopper and the lover of unique craftsmanship supremely executed, something that solves most gift-giving needs. It also offers to the smartly-gowned woman an indispensable adjunct to her costume that is both original and artistic. This particular hand bag is of red—an oft-found color in Greek embroideries. The handle is fashioned of the wood of the pear tree, a favorite one among the different orchard woods, which Miss Capps chooses for this purpose. It is interesting that among the orphan boys who have been instructed in this sort of handicraft since the Smyrna disaster Miss Capps has been able to establish in business two clever young craftsmen who carve and design from antique models, all the handles for bags, big and little, which the Near East Industries require.

No. 4—The design of this wall panel is a copy of a very ancient bedspread belonging to a private collection to which Miss Capps had special access as the daughter of one of the most brilliant of American scholars, Mr. Edward Capps PH. D., of Princeton University, a former United States Minister to Greece, now Chairman of the American School of Classical Studies in Athens. The original is in vivid red, its embroidery seeming in certain lights to be two-toned. Miss Capps in perpetuating, and in many cases restoring, old motifs long preserved only in museum pieces as a lost art, has given much intelligent attention to appropriate and accurate colors as well as designs. This particular work of art has been reproduced in the original tint and in a fascinating blue which is equally typical of its period, one of the best in Greek needlework.

No. 5—In Crete there is a handcraft movement similar to that of the Near East Industries. It is conducted for refugee orphans, and has many looms, which the interlocking projects of this work shop and those over which Miss Capps presides, enable her to utilize these advantages for her own designers and weavers. On this island, which is a very historic one in Greek history, the rarest sort of handicraft has prevailed from time immemorial. Here is shown a runner that not only attracts the eye and satisfies the sense of proportion, but claims attention by the beauty of its workmanship. It shows a traditional pattern that is a tradition in the Greek race. It depicts the currants from historic Corinth, sweet small grapes native to the Peloppanesian Peninsula that give ancient Corinth its name.

No. 6—Any eye can see that this kimono bridges Time itself in the interest of art. Here, finely woven cotton of a light weight suitable to feminine uses, is embroidered in motifs that still decorate the walls of the ancient palace of King Minas. These ducks are reproduced from designs on the walls of the bathroom which was as luxurious as any modern one in this age-old seat of royalty. Equally up-to-date models present fishes of various sorts woven into the material and interlaced with strange under-sea fishes and plants. The tulip pattern is extremely graceful also. For men there are dressing gowns in this same cotton weave but heavier, more masculine in effect. These have embroidered upon back and border crossed hatchets that give a decoratively beligerent air suitable to any husband, collegian or athlete.

Among other articles which the connoisseur will enjoy during this two-day sale is the natural colored tweed woven for winter resort wear, in both heavy and light weight silk, called "cocolarico" and spun and woven by the refugees. As it is without that shine which the thread of the cocoon customarily suggests, it looks like miraculously fine linen, except that it does not wrinkle, crush or lose its shape even through the roughest usage. This is a great boon to the traveler, the busy committee or business woman.

A tablecloth and runners of finest unbleached muslin, perfect for a seaside cottage or country home, are embroidered after the fashion of the Island of Skyros, where brides for centuries have embroidered their trousseaux in ships and in the queer denizens of the deep sea. This set is extremely attractive, and unlike any other anywhere save in Greece. Skyros besides being one of the most interesting of the islands of the Aegean, is also a point of pilgrimage for the traveler who wishes to pay tribute to Rupert Brooke, who died and is buried there—his tomb a shrine to the admirers of his poems and plays.

... tremely pretty, is once more at her post of Executive Secretary and indispensable to the comfort and pleasure of this membership.

Mrs. Horace Schmidlapp is returning today from a brief visit to New York, where she was called by the sudden death of an intimate friend of her family. She joined the Carl Schmidlapps in Manhattan and together they paid their trib- ... during her all-too-brief sojourn in Cincinnati.

JAMES MILLER McCUTCHEON IS CHRISTENED.

Mr. and Mrs. James McCracken McCutcheon, of New York, are the guests of Mrs. Clifford Miller, of the Hotel Alms, having come to Cincinnati this week-end especially ...

... Nicholas from 4:30 o'clock to 6 o'clock.

This hospitality will be an aftermath to the "School of Politics" and the luncheon meeting at the Netherlands Plaza, two important incidents of Republican Woman's Day in Cincinnati.

These cards bear the names of Mrs. George A. Wyeth, Mrs. Ellis A. Yost, Mrs. George Hoadly and Mrs. Leo Lindenberg, as the guests ...

... ican Association of University Women, the League of American Pen Women and the National Woman's Country Club.

Mrs. Hoadly, who as Representative from Ohio on the Executive Council of the National Republican Women's Club, has served on a number of its important committees, will have charge of the general arrangements for Republican Women's Day in Cincinnati.

... ident of the Cincinnati ... this national political ..., Mrs. Leo Lindenberg, ... a member of the Town ... of course, in her official ... reside at the business ... next Monday, and also ... Mrs. Brown's gracious ... tea.

On October 10–11, 1933, Louise Taft Semple opened her mansion on Pike Street in Cincinnati (now the Taft Museum) to host a display of handicrafts organized by Priscilla Capps. The *Cincinnati Enquirer* featured a long article that included images of some of the signature pieces of the NEI in Athens. (Retrieved from http://www.newspapers.com/)

... the Town Club to select a ticket.

Today at "Pokeway," her picturesque place on Turkey Foot Road, Mrs. Polk Laffoon is entertaining the Board of Governors of this now indispensable institution.

Miss Sherlock had a similar reunion a week or so ago, this series finishing the fiscal year of the Town Club which, opened on October 12, 1932, has had an amazing success during its first year.

Miss Mary Roberts, looking ex- ...

MRS. HARCOURT WELCOMED BY MANY FRIENDS.

An interesting and charming visitor in town is Mrs. Vivian Harcourt, of New York, who arrived on Saturday to spend a fortnight with her mother, Mrs. Joseph Wilshire, at the Vernon Manor. An agreeable succession of informal luncheon, teas and dinners are now being planned for Mrs. Harcourt by her many friends here who delight to make it pleasant for her ...

IN HONOR OF FEMININE REPUBLICAN LEADERS.

Invitations from "Duncarrick," the attractive residence in Dayton, Ohio, of Mrs. Katherine Kennedy Brown have just been received by the members of the Board of the Republican Women's Club and their out-of-town guests for the tea which this well-known Republican National Committeewoman from Ohio is giving on October 16, at the Town Club, atop the Sinton-St. ...

... the Republican Women of West Virginia immediately after the passage of the Nineteenth Amendment. For 12 years Mrs. Yost was a member of the West Virginia State Board of Education and is an active and honored trustee of West Virginia Wesleyan College, her alma mater, which in 1929 conferred upon her the honorary degree of L. H. D., as well as being a member of the Mortar Board fraternity, the D. A. R., the Amer- ...

...TEES FOR CHARITY BALL.

...Charity Ball, in the Hall ... at the Netherland Plaza ... er 24, Mrs. W. H. Albers ... ted the following com- ... Tickets, Mrs. Harry Anderson; Entertainment, Mrs. Walter Herschede; Supper, Mrs. Frederick Wallis Hinkle; Treasurer, Mrs. Edward Ballard; Secretary, Miss Mary Elizabeth Williams; Music, Mrs. Robert A. Cline; Floor, Mrs. C. C. Lambert; Junior Women's, Mrs. Charles A. Hinsch Jr.; Out of Town, Men's, Mr. Charles A. Hinsch Jr.; Poster Tea, Mrs. John J. Grau, co-Chairman, Miss Susanne Walsh; Decorations, Mrs. George McDonald; Junior Men's, Mr. Rich- ard Verkamp; General Chairman Men's Contact Committee, Mr. Harry Gilligan; Usher, Mrs. Frank Kunkel; Junior Men's Contact Committee, Mr. Richard Verkamp, Mr. Reginald Barnard, Mr. Andrew Hickenlooper Withrow, Mr. Andrew Foust Wiley, Mr. Charles Heekin, Mr. George Heekin, Mr. Raymond Kunkel. Miss Rosemary Hoppe is Chairman of the Poster Committee, and Mrs. Charles Williams is Chairman of the Box Committee; Invitations, Mrs. Louis Weber.

Miss Lucille Bardes, the interesting daughter of Mr. and Mrs. E. H. Bardes, has chosen the date of November 18 for her marriage to Mr. J. Richard Roe, of Elkhart, Indiana.

Initiating the agreeable succession of pre-nuptial hospitalities which is now being arranged in honor of these fiancees, Mrs. M. C. Farrell and Mrs. Dan Early combined forces for a surprise kitchen shower at the home of the latter on last Thursday evening.

Attached to each of the attractively tissued packages presented by some 40 friends of this bride-elect were clever bits of verse suitable to the occasion, some original and some selected from the writings of well-known poets.

Tht broadcasts of the Ohio Federation of Music Clubs, which were so popular a feature of this organization during the winter and early spring months, will again be resumed on Wednesday, October 11 at 2:30 o'clock over Station WFBE.

Tomorrow's program will include a duet for soprano and alto, in the old English style, a setting of the lyric of George Peele, a poet of the sixteenth century. It is called "Twice So Fair," the characters conversing being Aenone and Paris. It will be sung by Miss Amy Hattersley, soprano, and Mrs. Margo Topmoeller, mezzo-soprano, the composer. A solo, "To Her Piano," sung by Mrs. Ellen Laib, contralto, was written by Mrs. B. Y. Williams. A fantasie entitled "Contemplation," a trio, played by the Solens instrumental trio, Miss Helen Gough, violinist; Miss Winifred Hazlewood, cellist, and Mrs. Eleanor Wenning, pianist.

A Gypsy song, called "Romany Spring"— a poem by another Cincinnatian, Mrs. George Elliston, is another number of the music written by Miss Eleanor Wenning. It is sung by Miss Amy Hattersley, soprano, with Miss Eleanor Wenning at the piano. Miss Wenning dedicated this song to Miss Hattersley.

A quartet for women's voices, a nautical lullaby, dedicated to Mrs. John A. Hoffmann, who is presenting this program, is also included. It will be sung by Miss Dorothy Sieffermann, soprano; Miss Margo Topmoeller, mezzo-soprano; Miss Freda Meyer, contralto, and Miss Ellen Laib, contralto.

The final number on this program is of the composition of Miss Eleanor Wenning, a song for soprano with an obligato for two violins and 'cello. The title is "Prayer for Courage." This is sung and played by the Solens group, Miss Amy Hattersley, soprano; Miss Helen Gough, violin, and Miss Winifred Hazelwood, 'cello, and Miss Eleanor Wenning, piano, augmented by a second violin played by Miss Genevieve Bookwalter.

Mr. and Mrs. John C. Richardson's daughter, Miss Margaret Richardson, has chosen Saturday evening, November 4, as the date for her marriage to Dr. B. E. Boyer, the ceremony being quietly solemnized at 7:30 o'clock in the presence of the family connection and a few intimate friends of the bride and groom. Rev. Jesse Halsey will officate at the ritual.

Miss Eleanor Ellison, of Fort Thomas, will be the maid of honor, and Mr. Joseph Fossick, of Nashville, will be Dr. Boyer's best man.

Mrs. C. K. Ervin and Miss Blanche Yungblut inaugurated the prenuptial parties in honor of this bride-elect with a bridge party and surprise miscellaneous shower last week. Mrs. Lansing Speer gave a tea and hosiery shower last Friday afternoon in honor of Miss Richardson, who will be the center of interest also at the luncheon and bridge party which Mrs. Merritt Farrell will give on October 16 at her home on Belsaw Place, as well as at the bridge party and tea of which Mrs. Robert Adkins will be the hostess on October 19 at her home in Clifton.

The Kappa Kappa Gamma sorority will hold a memorial meeting on Friday evening, October 13, at the Kappa apartment in the Stratford Building in Clifton, in memory of Mrs. Alice Pillitson Barney, National President of the sorority, whose death occurred last week, and in tribute also to the late Mrs. Stanley M. Isaacs (Mary Baird), a member of the local chapter of this sorority who passed away recently.

The Sixth Street Chapter Notre Dame de Namur Alumnae will greet its newly-elected officers at a reception and tea, Saturday, November 14. Miss Dolores Brinker will be the new Vice President, Miss Helen Twomey, Corresponding Secretary; Miss Sara Molloy, Recording Secretary. Miss Brinker, a graduate also of the Sacred Heart College, received her M. A. degree at the University of Cincinnati last year. Miss Molloy is also a graduate of the Sacred Heart, and Miss Twomey of University of Cincinnati, and is active in the American Association of University Women.

This happy affair will take place at the Academy of Notre Dame on East Sixth Street, the hours being from 2 to 5 o'clock.

BALTIMORE BOY SOUGHT.

At the same time last night that police received a request from Baltimore, Md., police to help in locating a boy missing from that city Lillian White, 826 East Third Street, reported that her cousin, Albert Schnell, 11 years old, who has been missing from his home since October 2, was in the company of the Baltimore boy. The letter from Baltimore said that Charles Garrett, 15, had written to his parents from Cincinnati. Relatives of the Schnell boy said they traced the two boys to a down-town and a hilltop hotel, where the older boy registered as Greenfield Pitts. He had checked out of both hotels.

3c Marketing the Near East Industries in America

Beyond breaking even, the Near East Industries (NEI) aimed at being profitable, especially after the Near East Relief became the Near East Foundation (NEF). In 1930 James L. Barton, chair of the NEF, proudly noted that "eighteen thousand dollars' worth of these goods had been sold in a single season" mostly through sales aboard tourist ships. "From showing a monthly deficit," the operation had reached "the self-supporting stage." By the dawn of World War II the NEI in Greece had employed more than 2,000 women.

The NEI was represented in America by Rose Ewald, who marketed refugee crafts from the organization's flagship store at 151 Fifth Avenue in Manhattan. In 1930, when the NEF closed most of its outlet offices in America, an entrepreneurial New Yorker, Florence Spencer Duryea (1884–1966), conceived the idea of selling the NEI products through bazaars in private houses, clubs, and schools. In 1931 she raised the astonishing amount of $100,000 from the sale of refugee embroideries. Priscilla Capps traveled once a year to America to organize displays in various cities. Society women in New York, Cincinnati, Pittsburgh, and other U.S. cities would open their houses to Duryea or Capps so that they could display the NEI handicrafts. Louise Taft Semple in the 1930s hosted at least three such events in her mansion in Cincinnati.

Long promotional press releases published in U.S. newspapers presented the products of the NEI, educated the public about the value of preserving the folk art of Greece, and underscored the fact that this type of work gave employment to refugee women with dependent families. "Thus, under the American direction, the Greek women are eking out a living by embroidering for the American markets the traditional designs of their homeland."

N.V.B.

Handbag and table runner similar to (or the same as) the ones displayed at the Semple mansion in October 1933. The display also included a large doll (16.5 inches), similar to the one shown here, which was produced by the NEI (not in Greece). (ASCSA Archives, Jack L. Davis and April D. Michas Collections)

PITTSBURGH POST-GAZETTE: THURSDAY, APRIL 14, 1932

CLUBS ◆ NEWS OF INTEREST

At the Exhibit of Refugee Embroideries

—Post-Gazette Photos.

Name Hostesses For Chinese Art Exhibit and Tea

The hostesses for the benefit tea to be given Friday afternoon at the home of Mrs. George Oliver, Ellsworth avenue, by the Allegheny County League of Women Voters, will include Mrs. A. H. Bowman, chairman of the league committee; Mrs. Waldo Amos and Mrs. H. K. Griffiths. Assisting Mrs. Oliver, will be Mrs. Adam Jacobs, Mrs. F. O. Graham, Mrs. J. M. Simpson, Mrs. F. A. Bomb, Mrs. Bessie Kann Sacks and Mrs. H. D. Stark.

A group of young women who are to act as aides includes Miss Elizabeth Jenkins, Miss Catherine McCloskey, Miss Jane Bowman, Mrs. Edward J. McCrady, Mrs. Clark Kofover and Miss Betty Braun.

In connection with the tea, there will be a Chinese art exhibit, and among those who are sending art pieces are Mrs. Judson Crane, Mrs. Arthur E. Braun and Miss Myrtle McKendrick. Miss Mary T. Lang, who will speak on "Old Art in China," is bringing a most interesting collection. Mrs. E. O. Tabor will sing a group of songs in costume.

Jewish Juniors Give Supper Party For Anniversary

The Pittsburgh Section, National Council of Jewish Juniors will celebrate its tenth anniversary with a birthday supper-party, Monday evening, April 18, at 6:30 o'clock, in the Hotel Schenley.

The program committee consists of Sybil Goldman, chairman; Gladys Ziff, Helen Ginsberg, Yetta Azen Ravenna Alpert, Mrs. Louis Ruben, Ruth Berkman, Louise Cohen, Mrs. Aaron Jaffe, Deborah Feinberg, Ruth Grinberg and Alice Ferber.

Selections from the "Peer Gynt Suites" were chosen by Mrs. C. M. Laurie and her committee for the meeting of the Swissvale Woman's Club held Monday afternoon. Mrs. L. N. Smith gave a reading between numbers. Piano duets were played by Mrs. John A. Esler and Mrs. M. M. Chapman; Mrs. John R. Smith and Mrs. D. T. Price. Mrs. Hazel Martin was guest soloist. Mrs. Mathilde M. Chapman played a violin solo, and Mrs. C. M. Laurie gave a piano solo.

Mrs. J. R. Calihan, Mrs. C. L. Wilson and Mrs. Joseph N. Neid were appointed a nominating committee.

Past Matrons' Club O.E.S., Entertained By Retiring Leader

Mrs. A. R. Cook, of Brighton road, Northside, gave a beautifully appointed luncheon Monday, in the Italian room, William Penn Hotel, for the Past Matrons' Club of Allegheny Chapter, 106, Order of the Eastern Star. American beauty roses were used as table decorations and favors. Covers were laid for 17 guests. Honor guests were Mrs. H. G. Tench, a new member, and Mrs. William McConaghy, district deputy grand matron.

Mrs. Cook, president of the club, whose term of office had expired, presented the gavel to the incoming president, Mrs. Albert Vokach of Brookline, South Hills.

Mrs. John Howard Phillips of the Northside, is vice president. Miss Margaret Carson of the Northside, is secretary and treasurer.

The Homewood Woman's Club will hold its annual luncheon in the Arlington apartments, May 23. The club met Monday afternoon in the Homewood Carnegie Library with Mrs Stanley Johnston, chairman. Mrs. L. L. Hartley was leader and introduced Miss Suzanne Beatty who spoke on "The Child and the Law." Mrs. Beatty explained the laws of Pennsylvania for the protection and education of its children and also of the purpose and achievement of the juvenile court.

As a surprise, Class No. 17, of the Homewood Methodist Episcopal

On one of her drives to promote the NEI, Florence Spencer Duryea organized a sale at the house of Julia Dodge Rea of Pittsburgh. Rea was the daughter of Cleveland H. Dodge, a prominent figure in the administration of both the ARC and the NER. The *Pittsburgh Post-Gazette* featured photos of the sale. The long coat in the lower photo of the newspaper was among the items that Angeliki Hajimihali (1895-1965), the eminent Greek folklorist, included in the first volume of her *Greek Arts and Crafts* catalogue (1930). (Retrieved from http://www.newspapers.com)

Long coat produced by the NEI (Angeliki Hajimihali, "Embroideries and Hand-Woven Materials: Sample-Book" in *Greek Arts and Crafts* 1, Athens, 1930. ASCSA, Gennadius Library)

In addition to the handbags with string handles, the NEI in Athens launched a new series of bags with wooden handles made by orphans on Syros. (ASCSA Archives, April D. Michas Collection)

In the Kimport Dolls catalogue, *evzone* Demetrius was paired with a Greek peasant girl, Eleni, from Attica. (ASCSA Archives, Jack L. Davis Collection)

Inspired by ancient Greek mythology, the Bible, and local or exotic folklore, other pairs featured Odysseus and Penelope, Rebecca and Joseph of Jerusalem, Mitros and Philomela from Skyros, and Turks Ismet and Esme. "Esme looks from over her sheer veil upon a world of mosques and minarets, camels and caravans, for her native land is Arabia. [...] With her is reckless and dashing Ismet." (ASCSA Archives, Jack L. Davis Collection)

3D Doll Mania

"Ninety square feet of cloth is considered just enough for one pair of trousers" (according to the catalogue) for the festive garb of Perihan of Albania, who was paired with Hassan, "a dashing mountaineer known as one of the bold 'men of the eagle.'" Dark-eyed Jabel of Armenia, made by Armenian refugees in Greece, and lovely Yelena of Serbia supplemented the prosopography of Near Eastern dolls produced by NEI and marketed by Kimport. The Near East Foundation also supported doll production in Sofia, Bulgaria. They were slightly bigger (9 inches) than the average NEI dolls (8 inches) with faces made of plaster of Paris. On the right, next to the Kimport dolls are three examples: two versions of Sergei of Sofia (one produced by the NEI in Greece, the other by the NEF workshop in Sofia) and another doll of Bulgarian craftsmanship. (ASCSA Archives, Jack L. Davis Collection)

Despite the aggressive marketing of the Near East Industries (NEI), most Americans first fell in love with Greek dolls when they were advertised by Kimport Dolls, Inc., founded in 1935 in Independence, Missouri, to sell imported dolls from around the world. Kimport was managed by Ruby McKim (1891–1976), an artist, and her husband Arthur McKim (1891–1967), a marketing genius. Ruby is best remembered today as a quilter, especially for her Quaddy Quiltie block designs.

In 1935 Kimport contracted with Priscilla Capps to sell on commission 8-inch dolls dressed in traditional costumes of the Balkans and Near East, including Greece, Albania, Yugoslavia, Bulgaria, Palestine, and Arabia. Some 20 varieties were in circulation by the outbreak of World War II. Although Kimport usually required that a doll be made in the country represented by its costume, the NEI in Greece was exempted, since the women who manufactured the dolls there were refugees from the relevant countries.

Dolls were advertised through Kimport's catalogues, "Foreign Folk Dolls," and in a newsletter, "Doll Talk" (1936–1985). The same dolls were sold in the U.S. by the NEI itself, in bazaars, house parties, and at its flagship shop in Manhattan.

With Greece's entry into World War II, Priscilla Capps shifted the women in her workshops to the fabrication of supplies for the Greek army. Supply of the NEI dolls in the U.S. was largely exhausted by the start of 1941.

Two product lines by the NEI remain especially popular among collectors today—handbags and the dolls. Both can be found for sale on eBay and Etsy. The NEI items on display in this exhibition belong to collections presented to the ASCSA by Jack L. Davis, April D. Michas, and Julia L. Shear and Alexandra Shear.

J.L.D.

Kimport Dolls advertised its folk collections as "an investment in education." Hamilear of Montenegro's "tiny pill-box cap of red and black had a peculiar significance," the red standing "for blood shed in the struggle with the Turks," while the black was "in memory of Kossovo where the Serb empire was destroyed." (ASCSA Archives, Jack L. Davis Collection)

Kimport advertised its products through handsome catalogues which enticingly promoted the dolls as "Handmade in Athens" and offered them for sale for $4.00 (approximately $60–$70 in today's dollars). ("Foreign Folk Dolls," Independence, Missouri, 1939. ASCSA Archives, Jack L. Davis Collection)

HAMILEAR OF MONTENEGRO

FIVE centuries of heroic patriotism are embodied in Hamilear, and he portrays to the quick of his eyebrow a brave, handsome soldier. His costume is martial and gay with the pattern of braid on bolero and vest. A knee-length coat of felt flares below the girdled waist but can not quite conceal the enormous baggy-seated trousers. His tiny pill-box cap of red and black has a peculiar significance. The red stands for blood shed in the struggle with the Turks, while the black is in memory of Kossovo where the Serb empire was destroyed.

Would make handsome matching doll to Amalia

No. 867X—Hamilear, 8" $4.00

AMALIA OF THE GREEK COURT

AMALIA, a replica of the Greek Queen, has a regal beauty and stately mien which is set off by her charming costume of the Greek court. From the many romantic and picturesque styles in Greece, the official dress was chosen from Sparta, land of brave men and beautiful women. The skirt of a rich toned silk is delightfully feminine, but the jacket and matching bonnet are jauntily military. Her little pancake cap with its dangling beaded tassel and its insouciant angle makes its wearer quite irrisistible. Amalia is a Queenly little figure.

Exquisitely hand made in Athens.

No. 872X—Amalia, 8" Queen $4.00

Every Inch a Queen. Amalia is a Favorite in All Doll Circles

—24—

ELENI AND DEMETRIUS OF ATTICA

ELENI must be going to market for she carries a tiny handwoven basket and over one shoulder is slung a capacious homespun bag. Market day is also a day of courtship so she is looking her best in the colorful peasant dress, and the glossy wings of her hair are accentuated by the shawl which she has twisted so becomingly around her head. Beside her is a handsome young guard, Demetrius. With his short flared uniform and bright cap, he makes an escort of whom any girl might be proud.

These dolls were hand-made by native Greeks in Athens.

No. 859X—Demetrius, 8" g'd $4.00
No. 860X—Eleni, 8" peasant .. 4.00

SOPHIA AND YULKA OF MACEDONIA

THESE two girls possess a quaint appeal, due to the peculiar native finery of Macedonia. Sophia is softly hued, almost mid-victorian in pleated skirt and sheer blouse, with an incongruous damask apron and bizarre turban, elegantly tasseled. Yulka (not pictured) wears a helmet-like bonnet designed, they say, by Alexander the Great in recognition of their women's bravery. Her dark woolen costume is heavy with needlework. Both dolls are made with exquisite detail by Christian refugees.

Hand-Made In Greece

No. 854 —Sophia, 8" tall $4.00
No. 854A—Yulka, 8" tall 4.00

If You Want Any Special Doll We'll Try to Find it For You

—25—

"Every inch a Queen, Amalia is a favorite in all doll circles," according to the Kimport Dolls catalogue. Occasionally she was paired with King Otto. (ASCSA Archives, Jack L. Davis Collection)

The majority of the NEI dolls on display belong to the collection of Jack L. Davis, who has been systematically buying them from online marketplaces over the past decade. The Archives recently acquired another collection of dolls, as part of the Shear family papers, gifted to the ASCSA by Julia L. and Alexandra Shear. These dolls belonged to their grandparents, the archaeologist George Mylonas and his wife Lela Papazoglou. In addition to dolls produced by the NEI (above), the Mylonas collection includes similar but unlabeled dolls (below), larger in size (10 inches) and of higher quality, which could have been crafted by other dollmakers such as Despina Pappa-Paschalidou and her daughter Lili Paschalidou-Theodoridou. (ASCSA Archives, Ione M. and T. Leslie Shear Jr. Papers)

The Marathon Dam, 1932. (ASCSA Archives, Homer A. Thompson Papers)

4

PROMETHEAN PROJECTS

Copy of the Athenian Treasury at the Marathon Dam, 1932. (ASCSA Archives, Homer A. Thompson Papers)

4A The Marathon Dam

Hand in glove with U.S. humanitarian aid to Greece, commercial relations between the two countries expanded considerably in the 1920s. American contractors competed with the British in bidding for public works and won in many instances.

Until the 1920s, the city of Athens suffered from a water shortage which intensified after 1922. "You must understand, Mr. Prime Minister, that it is impossible for me to bathe and have tea on the same day," complained the American Minister in Greece in 1923, expressing his own point of view. In December 1924, amidst outrage by the British, Ulen & Company of Lebanon, Indiana, signed a contract with the Greek government to build the Marathon Waterworks: the dam, the Boyati tunnel, the city network, and the treatment facility.

Construction began in 1926 and was completed by 1931. The inaugural ceremony in 1931, in the presence of Prime Minister Eleftherios Venizelos, was an emotional experience for both Greeks and Americans.

Ulen & Company and its founder Henry Charles Ulen (1872–1963) were extremely proud of the Marathon Dam, not only for its engineering but also for its elegant appearance; it was the only marble-faced dam in the world. Conscious of its historic landscape and at the initiative of engineer Roy W. Gausmann (1882–1974), Ulen & Company constructed at the foot of the dam a small replica of the Athenian Treasury that Athens had erected at Delphi to commemorate her victory against the Persians in the Battle of Marathon (490 BCE).

To provide funds for the project the Greek state effected a loan of $10 million ($170 million today) in bonds. Though not officially classified as humanitarian aid, the Marathon project occupied a workforce of about 5,000 people—most of them refugees. Ulen built a town near the dam for the workers and cared for their diet, making sure that it was nutritionally rich. The company's "quasi-Fordist" paternalism was met with criticism from the trade unions. In later years, Ulen's good reputation in Greece gradually declined, after the Greek state's decision to label the tax levied for the dam's construction as the "Ulen tax."

N.V.B.

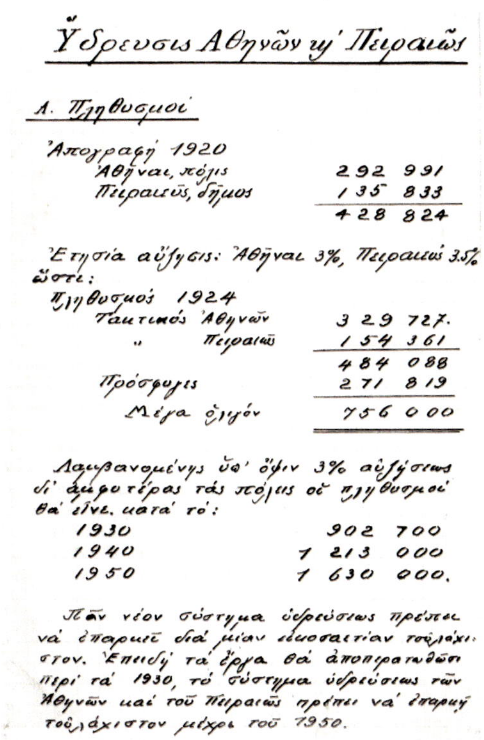

Ύδρευσις Αθηνών κ' Πειραιώς

Α. Πληθυσμοί

Απογραφή 1920

Αθήναι, πόλις	292 991
Πειραιεύς, δήμος	135 833
	428 824

Ετησία αύξησις: Αθήναι 3%, Πειραιεύς 3,5% ώστε:

πληθυσμός 1924

Ταυτικός Αθηνών	329 727.
" Πειραιώς	154 361
	484 088
Πρόσφυγες	271 819
Μέγα σύνολον	756 000

Λαμβανομένης υπ' όψιν 3% αυξήσεως δι' αμφοτέρας τας πόλεις οι πληθυσμοί θα είναι κατά το:

1930	902 700
1940	1 213 000
1950	1 630 000.

Παν νέον σύστημα υδρεύσεως πρέπει να επαρκεί διά μίαν εικοσαετίαν τουλάχιστον. Επειδή τα έργα θα αποπερατωθούν περί τα 1930, το σύστημα υδρεύσεως των Αθηνών και του Πειραιώς πρέπει να επαρκή τουλάχιστον μέχρι του 1950.

The studies of two Greek engineers with international experience, Theologos Genidounias (1871–1938) and Petros Loprestis (1871–1941), formed the basis for the work executed by Ulen & Company. Personal notes of Theologos Genidounias about the water problem of Athens, ca. 1925. (ASCSA Archives, Constantine Vovolinis Papers, Theologos Genidounias folder)

From the inauguration of the Marathon Dam in 1931. *Above:* people from the local community watch the event. *Below:* Greek president Pavlos Koundouriotis and prime minister Eleftherios Venizelos, in the company of engineer and Ulen manager Roy W. Gausmann, 1931. (ERT Archives, Petros Poulides Collection)

Illustrated article about the Marathon Dam in *L'Illustration*, December 31, 1932. (ASCSA Archives, Constantine Vovolinis Papers)

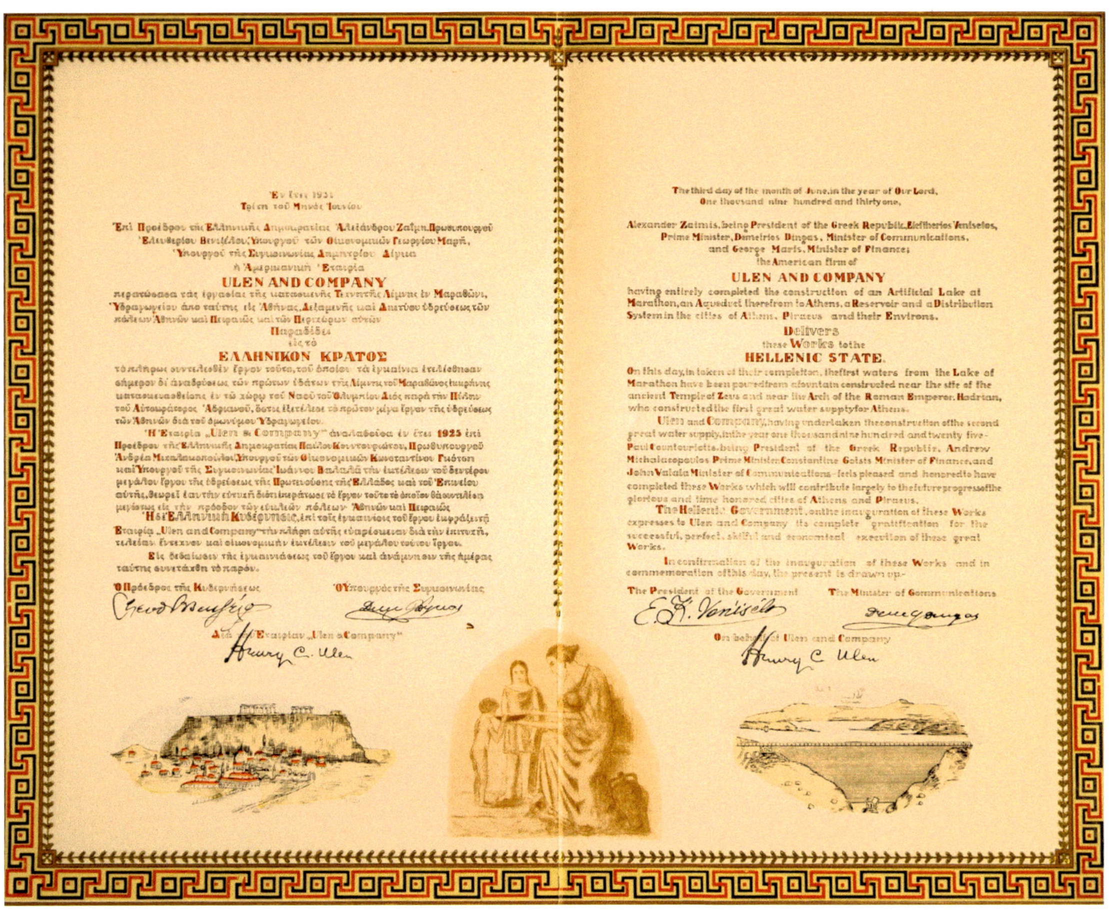
ULEN AND COMPANY

ΕΛΛΗΝΙΚΟΝ ΚΡΑΤΟΣ

The third day of the month of June, in the year of Our Lord, One thousand nine hundred and thirty one,

Alexander Zaimis, being President of the Greek Republic, Eleftherios Veniselos, Prime Minister, Demetrios Dingas, Minister of Communications, and George Maris, Minister of Finance; the American firm of

ULEN AND COMPANY

having entirely completed the construction of an Artificial Lake at Marathon, an Aqueduct therefrom to Athens, a Reservoir and a Distribution System in the cities of Athens, Piraeus and their Environs.

Delivers these Works to the

HELLENIC STATE.

On this day, in token of their completion, the first waters from the Lake of Marathon have been poured from a fountain constructed near the site of the ancient Temple of Zeus and near the Arch of the Roman Emperor, Hadrian, who constructed the first great water supply for Athens.

Ulen and Company, having undertaken the construction of the second great water supply, in the year one thousand nine hundred and twenty five - Paul Countouriotis, being President of the Greek Republic, Andrew Michalacopoulos Prime Minister, Constantine Goists Minister of Finance, and John Valala Minister of Communications - feels pleased and honored to have completed these Works which will contribute largely to the future progress of the glorious and time honored cities of Athens and Piraeus.

The Hellenic Government, on the inauguration of these Works expresses to Ulen and Company its complete gratification for the successful, perfect, skilful and economical execution of these great Works.

In confirmation of the inauguration of these Works and in commemoration of this day, the present is drawn up-

The President of the Government — E. K. Veniselos

The Minister of Communications — Dingas

On behalf of Ulen and Company — Henry C. Ulen

In 1940 Roy W. Gausmann, engineer and assistant manager of the Marathon project, prepared and distributed a 300-page personal memoir, titled *Water for Athens*, with his own drawings. The memoir included a copy of the delivery document signed by prime minister Venizelos and Henry C. Ulen on June 3, 1931. (Roy W. Gausmann, *Water for Athens*, Athens, 1940. ASCSA, Gennadius Library)

The Lion of Amphipolis, 1938. In 1942, the Lion of Amphipolis featured on a 1,000 drachma note issued by the Bank of Greece. (ASCSA Archives, Archaeological Photographic Collection)

4B The Reclamation of Strymon and Drama Valleys

The Greek government's agreement with the Refugee Settlement Commission in 1923 stipulated that 500,000 hectares of land be provided to Asia Minor refugees. After the Balkan Wars (1912–1913) and the exchange of the Greek and Turkish populations (1923), there was available land in Macedonia. Since much of it was swampy and not arable, substantial bonification projects were needed. The reclamation of the Strymon and the Drama valleys in Eastern Macedonia was assigned to the American companies John Monks & Sons and Ulen & Company on October 20, 1928, after a long period of negotiation. The total cost of the project came to about $19 million (approximately $300 million today), and it employed 3,800 people. Two Greek engineers, Theologos Genidounias, on behalf of Monks-Ulen, and Petros Loprestis, representing the Greek state, were also involved.

The Strymon Valley project included dredging and damming the river, creating an artificial reservoir (Lake Kerkini), and building bridges and roads. During these operations in 1929, the workmen rediscovered the marble fragments of a large lion monument along the banks of the river. The initiative to reassemble the monument belonged to two engineers of the Monks-Ulen Company, Roy W. Gaussman and William Judge, who, in 1933, enlisted the support of the new U.S. Minister in Greece, Lincoln MacVeagh. In collaboration with French archaeologists, who were excavating at nearby Philippi, and with help from the American School of Classical Studies at Athens, MacVeagh launched a fundraising campaign which ultimately covered the cost of the reconstruction. With contributions from American philhellenes and many Greeks, the reconstruction of the Lion of Amphipolis was completed in 1937. Swedish-American archaeologist Oscar Broneer and conservator Andreas Panayotakis were responsible for the execution of the project.

N.V.B.

Fragments of the marble lion discovered during the dredging of the Strymon River, ca. 1929. (ASCSA Archives, Oscar Broneer Papers)

Maps showing the plains of Serres and Drama before and after their drainage. (ASCSA Archives, Constantine Vovolinis Papers, Theologos Genidounias folder)

The restoration of the Lion of Amphipolis in progress, ca. 1936. The lion on the left is a plaster cast. (ASCSA Archives, Oscar Broneer Papers)

ΤΙΜΗ ΕΚΑΣΤΟΥ ΦΥΛΛΟΥ ΔΡΑΧΜΗ ΜΙΑ

ΠΡΟΟΔΟΣ
ΤΩΝ ΑΘΗΝΩΝ

ΤΕΤΑΡΤΗ
2
ΦΕΒΡΟΥΑΡΙΟΥ 1927
Τῆς Ὑπαπαντῆς

ΣΥΝΔΡΟΜΑΙ
ΕΣΩΤΕΡΙΚΟΥ ΔΡΑΧΜΑΙ 400 – ΕΥΡΩΠΗΣ £ 3
ΕΞΑΜΗΝΟΣ » 200 – ΑΜΕΡΙΚΗΣ $ 15

ΤΗΣ ΗΜΕΡΑΣ
ΤΕΤΑΡΤΗ 2 Φεβρουαρίου 1927

Η ΓΕΡΟΥΣΙΑ

Παρὰ τὰς ἀντιρρήσεις τῶν ...ο κομμάτων τῆς ἀντιβενιζε...κῆς παρατάξεως καὶ μερικὰς ...τως διαφωτιστικὰς ἀγορεύ...ς ὡρισμένων βουλευτῶν καὶ ... τοῦ κ. Ν. Κολλυβᾶ, ὁ θε...ὸς τῆς Γερουσίας ἐψηφίσθη, ...ότι τὸν ἠθέλησεν ὁ βενιζελι...ός. Θὰ ἦτο ἀνιαρὸν ὅθεν νὰ ...απτυχθῇ ἐκ νέου συζήτησις ... τοῦ ζητήματος. Γεννᾶται ...ως ἡ ἀπορία: τί θὰ συμβῇ ἂν ...θεσμὸς οὗτος χρεωκοπήσει, ὡς ...κμένεται μετὰ βεβαιότητος ...ὼς θὰ δυνηθῇ ἡ Χώρα νὰ ἀ...λλαγῇ αὐτοῦ, ἐφόσον θὰ ἔχῃ ...ράσῃ εἰς τὸ Σύνταγμα; Του...χιστον ἂς καταβληθῇ εἰλικρι...ς προσπάθεια ἀπὸ μέρους τῶν ...μμάτων νὰ ἐπιτευχθῇ συγ...ότησις τοῦ νέου τούτου Σώ...τος ἀρτία, ὄχι ἐπὶ τῇ βάσει ...μματικῶν ὑπολογισμῶν καὶ ...νοποιήσεων, ἀλλὰ μὲ πνεῦμα ...νικώτερον, ἐθνοπρεπὲς καὶ ...βαρῶς ἐπιστημονικόν. Διότι

ΠΛΟΥΤΟΠΑΡΑΓΩΓΙΚΑ ΖΗΤΗΜΑΤΑ
ΤΑ ΥΔΡΑΥΛΙΚΑ ΕΡΓΑ
ΤΗΣ ΠΕΔΙΑΔΟΣ ΤΩΝ ΣΕΡΡΩΝ ΚΑΙ ΤΟΥ ΠΟΤΑΜΟΥ ΣΤΡΥΜΩΝΟΣ

ΑΡΘΡΟΝ ΤΟΥ ΜΗΧΑΝΙΚΟΥ κ. Θ. ΓΕΝΙΔΟΥΝΙΑ

Τὰ ὑδραυλικὰ ἔργα τῆς πεδιάδος Σερρῶν καὶ τοῦ ποταμοῦ Στρυμῶνος δὲν ἐμελετήθησαν ἐν τῷ συνόλῳ αὐτῶν, ἢ κατ' ἐντολὴν τῆς ἑλληνικῆς Κυβερνήσεως παρὰ τοῦ ἀγγλικοῦ Οἴκου Τζῶν Τζάκσον, παγκοσμίου μὲν φήμης, διαλυθέντος ὅμως ἤδη μετὰ τὸν θάνατον τοῦ ἀρχηγοῦ αὐτοῦ. Ἡ σχετικὴ μελέτη ὑπεβλήθη ἐν ἔτει 1922, ἐξεπονήθη δὲ ὑπὸ τὴν ἄμεσον ἐπίβλεψιν τοῦ κ. Α. Οὐίτλεϋ, εἰδικοῦ καὶ λίαν πεπειραμένου περὶ τὰ τοιαῦτα ἔργα μηχανικοῦ.

Τὴν ἀνωτέρω μελέτην παρηκολούθησα ἤδη κατὰ τὴν ἐκπόνησιν αὐτῆς καὶ ἐξήλεγξα ἐπανειλημμένως. Τὰ ἐξ αὐτῆς ὑποβαλλόμενα πορίσματα κα... [illegible]

σχεδὸν καθ' ὁλοκληρίαν καὶ χρησιμοποιῶ ἐν μέρει ἐν τῷ παρόντι ἄρθρῳ.

Προκειμένου περὶ ἔργων προοριζομένων, ἀφ' ἑνὸς μὲν πρὸς προστασίαν 1.200.000 στρεμμάτων κατακλυζομένων ἐκ πολλῶν σημείων συγχρόνως ὑπὸ ὑδάτων πλέον

μετρον 5,0 ἔναντι 6,0 μέχρις 7,0 σήμερον κατὰ τὰς μεγίστας δὲ πλημμύρας θὰ ἀνέρχεται εἰς ὑψόμετρον 6,0 ἔναντι 8,0 σήμερον. Ἡ μεταξὺ τῶν ὑψομέτρων 4,0 καὶ 6,0 χωρητικότης τῆς λίμνης εἶνε 100 ἑκ. κ. μ., εἰς τρόπον ὥστε δύναται νὰ ἐναποθηκευθῇ

Ἡ διευθέτησις τῆς πεδινῆς κοίτης τοῦ Στρυμῶνος δύναται νὰ ἐπιτευχθῇ διὰ τῶν ἑξῆς τριῶν τρόπων:

1) Διὰ τῆς ἐκσκαφῆς νέας κοίτης ἀκολουθούσης τὰς κοίτας τῆς Μπελίκας καὶ τοῦ Μαιάνδρου καὶ ἐκεῖθεν διὰ τῶν ἑλῶν βορείως τοῦ Ταχινοῦ μέχρι τῆς λίμνης ταύτης. Κόστος κατασκευῆς 10,655,000 μετ. δρχ.

2) Διὰ τῆς χρησιμοποιήσεως τῆς ὑπαρχούσης κοίτης μέχρι χιλ. 37,5 καὶ ἐκεῖθεν διὰ τῆς ἐκσκαφῆς νέας κοίτης διερχομένης περὶ τὰ χωρία Κουκουλοὺκ καὶ Γενίκιοϊ μέχρι τῆς Μπελίκας καὶ τοῦ Μαιάνδρου. Ἐκεῖθεν ὡς καὶ προηγουμένως. Κόστος κατασκευῆς 2[illegible],500,000 μετ. δρχ.

3) Διὰ τῆς χρησιμοποιήσεως τῆς λίμνης Μπουτκόβου πρὸς ἐναποθήκευσιν τῶν ὑδάτων πλημμυρῶν (χωρητικότης μεταξὺ ὑψομέτρων 27 καὶ 29, 68 ἑκ. κ. μ.) ὁπόθεν τὰ ὕδατα θὰ ἀκολουθοῦν μέχρι χιλ. 37.5 τὴν ὑπάρχουσαν κοίτην. Ἀπὸ τοῦ σημείου τούτου ἡ κοίτη διευθετεῖται κατὰ τὸν ἀνωτέρω τρόπον ἀριθ. 2. Κόστος κατασκευῆς 28,000,000 μετ. δρχ.

Ἡ προτίμησις πρέπει νὰ δοθῇ εἰς τὸν τρόπον διευθετήσεως ἀριθ. 1 ἕνεκα τῶν ἀκολούθων λόγων.

Ἡ νέα κοίτη τοποθετεῖται εἰς τὴν ἐνδεδειγμένην θέσιν διὰ τὴν μόνην ἀποχετευτικὴν τάφρον τῆς πεδιάδος, ἤτοι εἰς τὴν χαμηλο-

δύναται νὰ διοχετεύσῃ 2800 κ. μ. ἀνὰ δευτερόλεπτον.

Κατὰ τὴν διάβασιν τῆς κοίτης διὰ τῶν χθαμαλωτέρων ἐκτάσεων δὲν ἀπαιτεῖται ἐκσκαφὴ ἢ μόνον πρὸς κατασκευὴν τῶν αναχωμάτων. Εἰς τὰς ὑψηλότερον κειμένας περιφερείας προβλέπεται ἡ ἐκσκαφὴ κοίτης πλάτους 60 μέχρι 200 μέτρων, ἀναλόγως τοῦ ὑψομέτρου τοῦ διασχιζομένου ἐδάφους. Ἡ μεταξὺ τῶν ἀναχωμάτων ἀπόστασις ποικίλλει μεταξὺ 300 καὶ 500 μέτρων, τὸ δὲ ὕψος αὐτῶν μεταξὺ 2.2 καὶ 3.5 μέτρων. Τὸ ὁλικὸν μῆκος τῆς νέας κοίτης μέχρι τῆς λίμνης Ταχινοῦ εἶνε 60.545 μ[illegible], ἔναντι [illegible]

Διὰ στάθμην ὕδατος 6,0 ἐντὸς τῆς λίμνης, ὁ μέσος ὅρος τῆς κλίσεως τῆς ἐπιφανείας τοῦ ὕδατος εἶνε 1:1084 ἔναντι 1:1575 σήμερον.

Ἡ νέα κοίτη τοῦ Στρυμῶνος τέμνει ἀριθμόν τινα ὑπαρχουσῶν ῥοῶν. Πρὸς περισυλλογὴν τούτων ἐκσκάπτεται παραλλήλως πρὸς τὸ ἀριστερὸν ἀνάχωμα τάφρος, δι' ἧς τὰ ὕδατα τῶν ῥοῶν τούτων περισυλλέγονται καὶ διοχετεύονται μέχρι τῆς ἀνωτέρω ἀναφερθείσης ἀντιπλημμυρικῆς τάφρου τοῦ Φερχανλῆ.

2) Μερικὴ ἀποξήρανσις τῆς λίμνης Μπουτκόβου. — Ἅμα τῇ ἐκτροπῇ τοῦ Στρυμῶνος εἰς τὴν νέαν αὐτοῦ κοίτην, ἡ ἀποχέτευσις τῶν ὑδάτων ἐκ τῆς λίμνης τοῦ Μπουτκόβου καθίσταται εὔκολος διὰ τῆς ἐκσκαφῆς τά-

Newspaper article by engineer Theologos Genidounias in support of reclamation works in the Strymon Valley, *Πρόοδος*, February 2, 1927. (ASCSA Archives, Constantine Vovolinis Papers, Theologos Genidounias folder)

A Princely Gift to the American School of Classical Studies, Athens

His Excellency, Mr. Gennadius, Dean of the Diplomatic Service of the Kingdom of Greece, Has Given His Library of 50,000 Rare Volumes and Supplementary Collections; and William Caleb Loring of Boston, President of the Board of Trustees, in a Letter to the Donor, Says: "Greece Is Obviously the Most Appropriate Home for Your Remarkable Collection, and Greece, as Well as America, Is Equally Delighted"

By THEODORE G. JOSLIN

4c The Gennadius Library

A few weeks before the conflagration of Smyrna in 1922, Joannes Gennadius (1844–1932), retired Minister of Greece to the Court of St. James, offered his collection of 30,000 books to the American School of Classical Studies at Athens in a permanent trust "as a token of his admiration for the United States, [this] great country," with the understanding that the School would build a home for the collection and hire staff to maintain the library for the use of professors and scholars.

On land assigned by the Greek government to the American School, and thanks to a generous grant of $275,000 donated by the Carnegie Corporation, the New York architects John Van Pelt and W. Stuart Thompson began construction of the elegant neoclassical library in 1923. At the American School there are detailed records about the cost of the project (materials and labor), also documenting its difficulties because of inflation, political turmoil, and strikes. In the three years of construction hundreds of refugees in need of work were employed.

Gennadius hoped that his library would enable the American School "to become a world centre for the study of Greek history, literature, and art, both ancient Byzantine and modern." Focusing on the study of Byzantium and modern Greece, historical periods that were still developing as disciplines in the 20th century, the academic expertise of the Gennadius librarians indeed broadened the scope of the American School by expanding its academic offerings and by providing a research home for all those who partake in Greek education. Gennadius's legacy has nurtured many scholars from all over the world expanding the horizons of Hellenic studies.

M.G.

Opposite: Exterior view of the Gennadius Library with the griffon, June 30, 1925. (ASCSA, Gennadius Library, Joannes Gennadius Scrapbook)

Gennadius Library facade and inscription.

Clarinda Buck, wife of ASCSA annual professor Carl Darling Buck, plants the first tree, a cypress, in the Gennadeion gardens, January 4, 1924.

(ASCSA, Gennadius Library, Joannes Gennadius Scrapbook)

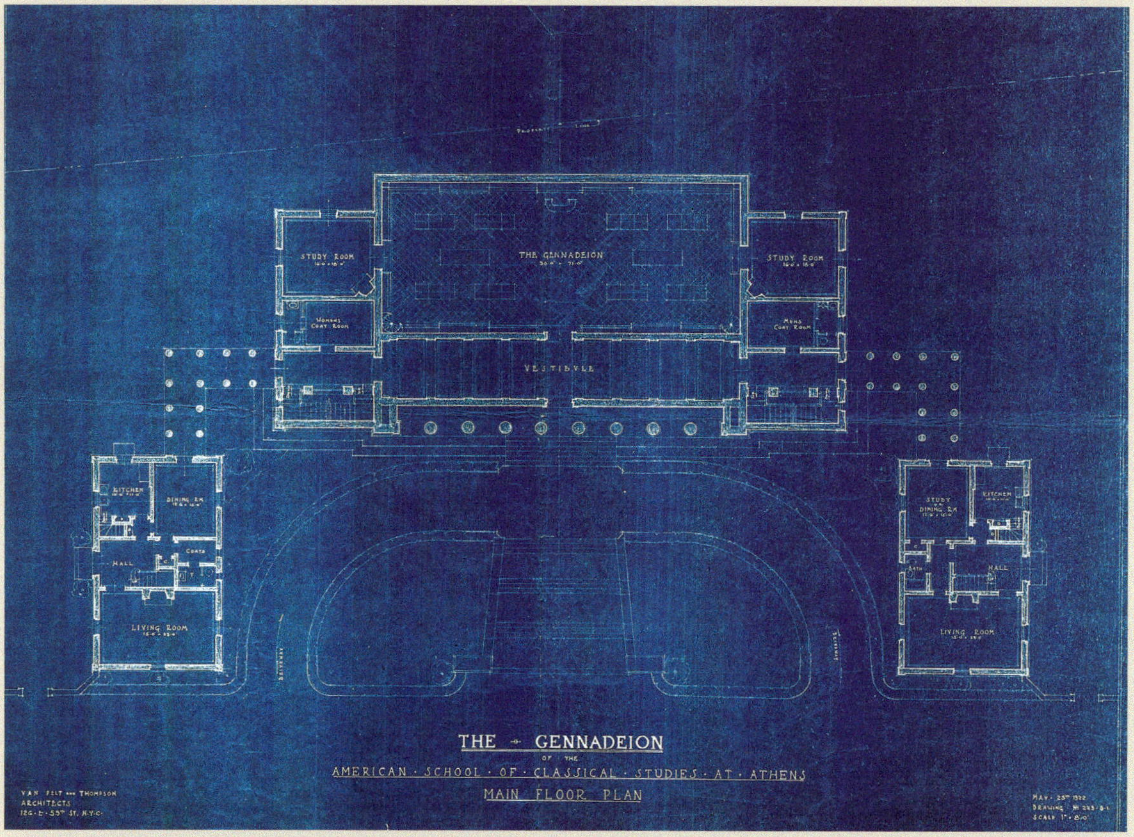

John Van Pelt and W. Stuart Thompson, plan of the Gennadius Library, main floor, May 25, 1922. (ASCSA Archives)

Thanksgiving dinner for the workmen, November 29, 1923. (ASCSA, Gennadius Library, Joannes Gennadius Scrapbook)

"The Gennadeion Library at Athens, Van Pelt and Thompson, Architects," article published in *Architecture and Building* 58/9, September 1926.

Address of Joannes Gennadius at the opening of the library, April 23, 1926.

(ASCSA, Gennadius Library, Joannes Gennadius Scrapbook)

From
Hellenic Information Bureau
Investment Bldg. Washington, D. C.

September

ARCHITECTURE
AND BUILDING

PUBLISHED BY THE WILLIAM T. COMSTOCK COMPANY NEW YORK
30c A COPY $3.00 A YEAR

ARCHITECTURE AND BUILDING. Plate 169

THE GENNADEION LIBRARY, ATHENS, GREECE
Van Pelt & Thompson, Architects.

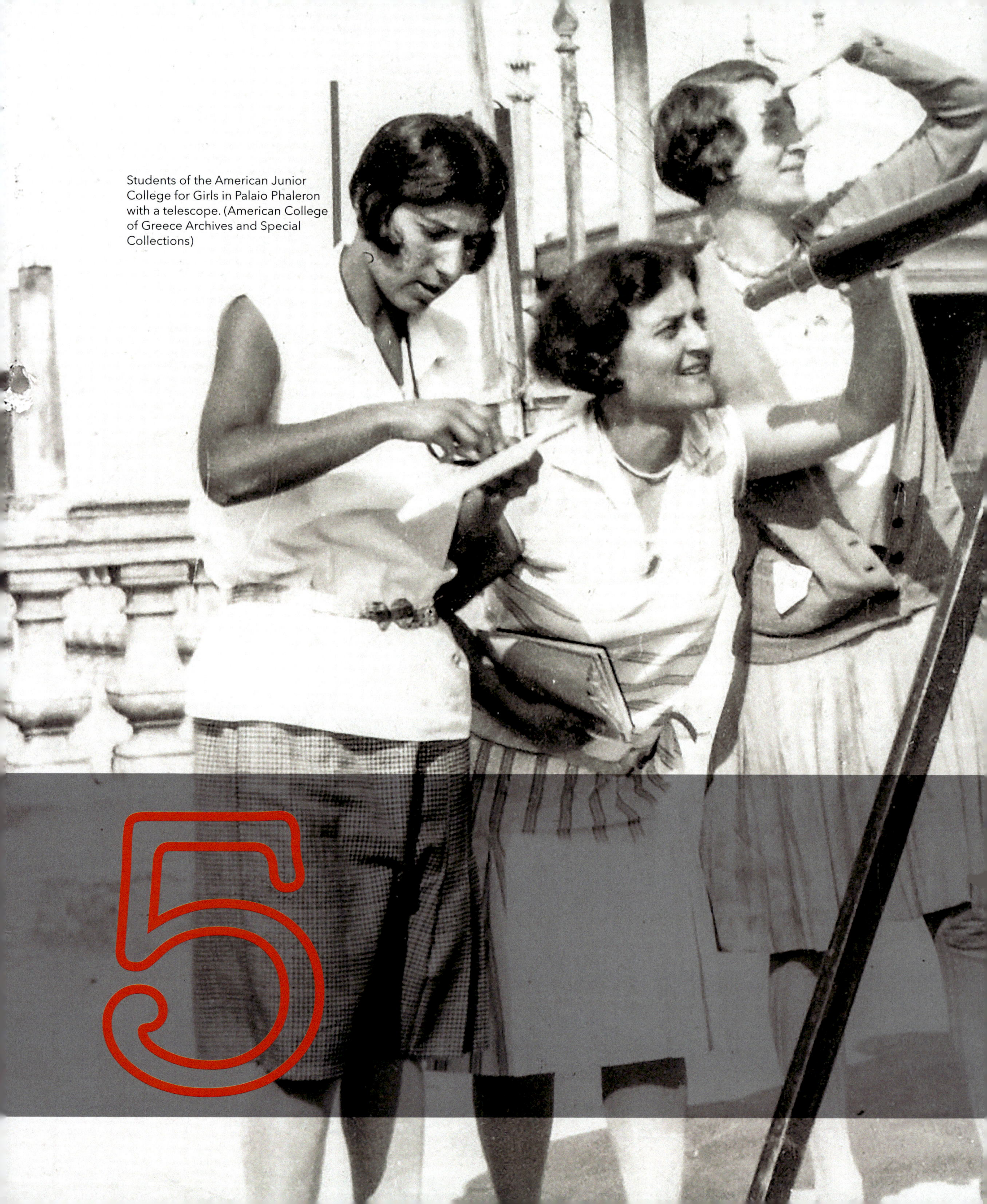

Students of the American Junior College for Girls in Palaio Phaleron with a telescope. (American College of Greece Archives and Special Collections)

5

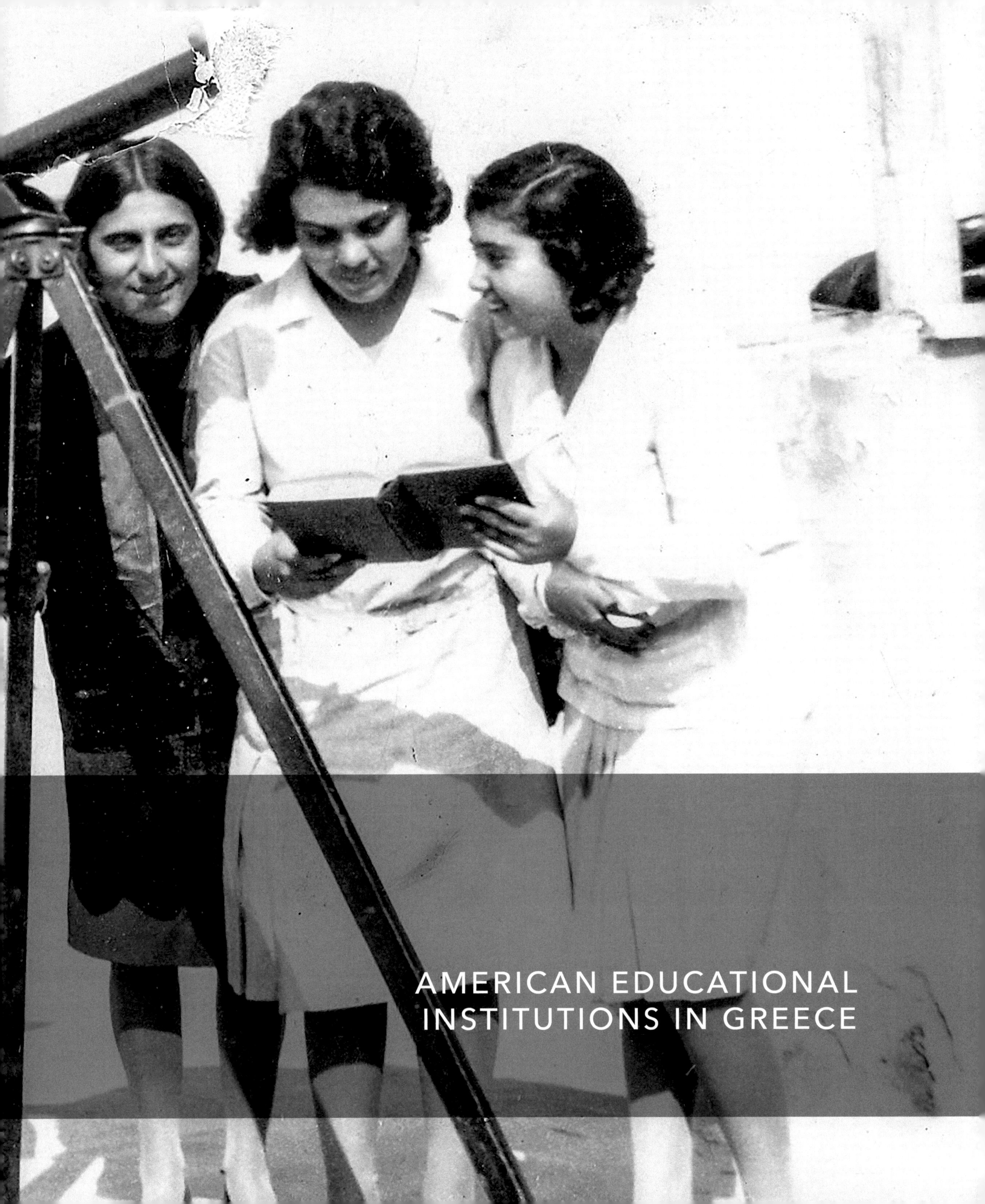
AMERICAN EDUCATIONAL
INSTITUTIONS IN GREECE

Students of the American Junior College for Girls helping the Feed the Children Society. (American College of Greece Archives and Special Collections)

5A Bringing Liberal Arts Education to Greece

Education was one of the most important Protestant missionary initiatives. From the late 19th century, the American Board of Commissioners for Foreign Missions and the Women's Board of Missions had maintained important schools for Christians in the Ottoman Empire.

These schools had to adapt to the new world order that followed the end of World War I, in tandem with the rise of the research university and an increase in vocational subjects taught in the U.S.

Despite the skepticism of the Greek Orthodox Church vis-à-vis their proselytizing, American schools were encouraged to operate in Greece by Eleftherios Venizelos with promises of land concessions and tax exemptions. Having modified their curriculum to offer a secular education conforming to the mandates of the new Greek educational law, these schools played a pivotal role in Greece by offering new paradigms of instruction and learning on the model of the principles of liberal arts colleges. Sports, libraries, and a strong work ethic strengthened the character and individual abilities of graduates, setting them apart from their peers and making them desirable members of Greek society. In this way, the American schools functioned as a mechanism for empowering refugees and strengthening society in general.

Three venerable American educational institutions continued to operate and transferred their activities to Greece: the American Junior College for Girls in Athens, and Anatolia College and the American Farm School in Thessaloniki. Their lasting success speaks to the important role they played in the formation of a Greek bourgeois elite in the last century.

Refugee barracks in Thessaloniki, ca. 1925. (Anatolia College Archives and Special Collections)

True to the missionary ideals of their founders, along with the Young Men's Christian Association (YMCA) and Young Women's Christian Association (YWCA), these institutions played an important role in providing solace and education to refugees after 1922.

M.G.

Harvesting, June 1926. (American Farm School Historical Archives)

5B The American Farm School

The American Farm School (AFS) was founded in the outskirts of Thessaloniki in 1904 by American missionary John Henry House and his wife, Susan Adeline, to provide a modern education to young boys so that they could become leaders in agriculture. Hands-on training in field and garden crops, vineyards and orchards, livestock, and silkworm production, and in industrial arts such as carpentry, masonry, and blacksmithing, prepared American Farm School graduates for success in farming and, over time, for contributing to the economic development of Greece.

House and his son, Charles Lucius House, who was director of the AFS from 1929 to 1955, dedicated their lives to "educating the whole individual: the head, the hands, the heart." Many of their first students were orphan boys. In total, from 1921 to 1938, there are 164 records of students whose place of birth was a region of Turkey.

The staff of AFS provided shelter, aid, and medical care to refugees. The construction of Princeton Hall, a dormitory for orphaned refugee children, brought to the campus about a thousand refugee workers. By 1924 the American Farm School and its students, in collaboration with the British Society of Friends, the Bible Lands Mission Aid Society, and the League of Nations Commission, were working with refugees within a radius of about 50 kilometers from the school's facilities, a total of 50 villages with 300 families.

M.G.

An AFS student demonstrates the straight tooth harrow during Demonstration Day, June 1929. (American Farm School Historical Archives)

AFS class photo, 1926. Charles House is seen on the left. (American Farm School Historical Archives)

Princeton Hall, a dormitory for orphaned refugee children at AFS, which began to be built by 1,000 refugees in December 1922. (American Farm School Historical Archives)

Publicity for the gambusia fish that eats the larvae of the anopheles mosquito. Thanks to AFS director Henry House, the small fish was imported from Rome to be grown as a weapon against malaria.

Tractor. Demonstration Day, June 1929.

(American Farm School Historical Archives)

5c The American Junior College for Girls

The American Collegiate Institute for Girls (ACI), currently the American College of Greece (ACG), was founded in Smyrna in 1875 by a missionary from Massachusetts, Maria West. Its goal was to liberate women from the slavery of illiteracy. Its motto, "Non ministrari sed ministrare" (to serve and not to be served), defines the character and values of the college.

In the aftermath of the Smyrna Catastrophe, the dean of the ACI in Smyrna, Minnie Mills (1872–1965), managed to secure safe passage to Athens for her students. In a few weeks, the staff that had arrived in Athens established the ACI Relief Committee, which assisted refugees from its base in the villa Skouloudi in Piraeus. One of the most significant activities of the Athens station of the American Board of Commissioners for Foreign Missions and the ACI Relief Committee was the operation of small schools and hospitals, and the provision of Bible lessons, especially for Armenians in the refugee "villages" of Dourgouti and Kokkinia.

The following year, Mills and the school principal, Emily McCallum (1858–1956), reopened the college as the American Junior College for Girls in the Palaio Phaleron district of Athens. The first class comprised 88 students: Armenians, Greeks, and one American girl; 73 were refugees from Asia Minor, Pontus, and Russia. Minnie Mills served as the college principal from 1928 to 1932 and its president until 1940 and made the school one of the leading teaching institutions in the country.

In 1932 a new campus was opened in the Hellenikon area of Athens, and in 1965 the school moved to Ayia Paraskevi where it is still located.

M.G.

Opposite: The first building of the American Junior College for Girls school at Palaio Phaleron, date unknown.

Minnie Mills in her office, date unknown.

(American College of Greece Archives and Special Collections)

Students of the American Junior College for Girls during an excursion by the sea, date unknown. (American College of Greece Archives and Special Collections)

Flora Haniotou, director of the Boarding Department (1948–1979) of the American Junior College for Girls, with students in the common room of the Hill House at Pierce College, Hellenikon campus, 1950. (American College of Greece Archives and Special Collections)

An American College for Women in Ancient Smyrna

"Where there is neither Jew nor Greek, Barbarian nor Scythian, but all are one."

Brochure of the American College for Women in Smyrna, 1922. (American College of Greece Archives and Special Collections)

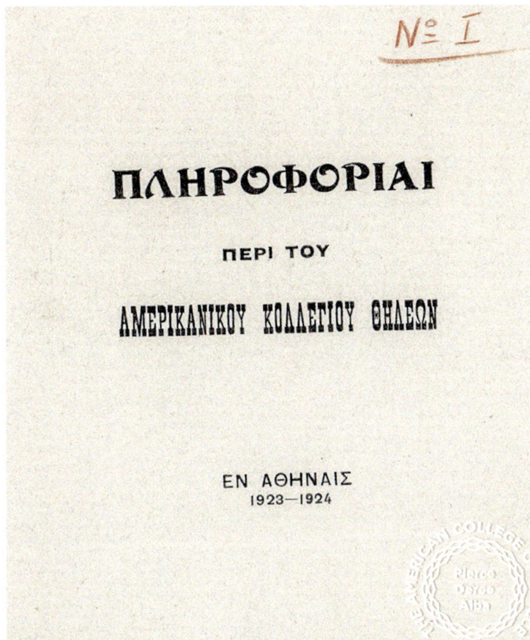

№ I

ΠΛΗΡΟΦΟΡΙΑΙ

ΠΕΡΙ ΤΟΥ

ΑΜΕΡΙΚΑΝΙΚΟΥ ΚΟΛΛΕΓΙΟΥ ΘΗΛΕΩΝ

ΕΝ ΑΘΗΝΑΙΣ

1923—1924

First catalogue of the American Junior College for Girls, 1923-1924.

Students of the American Junior College for Girls playing basketball, date unknown.

(American College of Greece Archives and Special Collections)

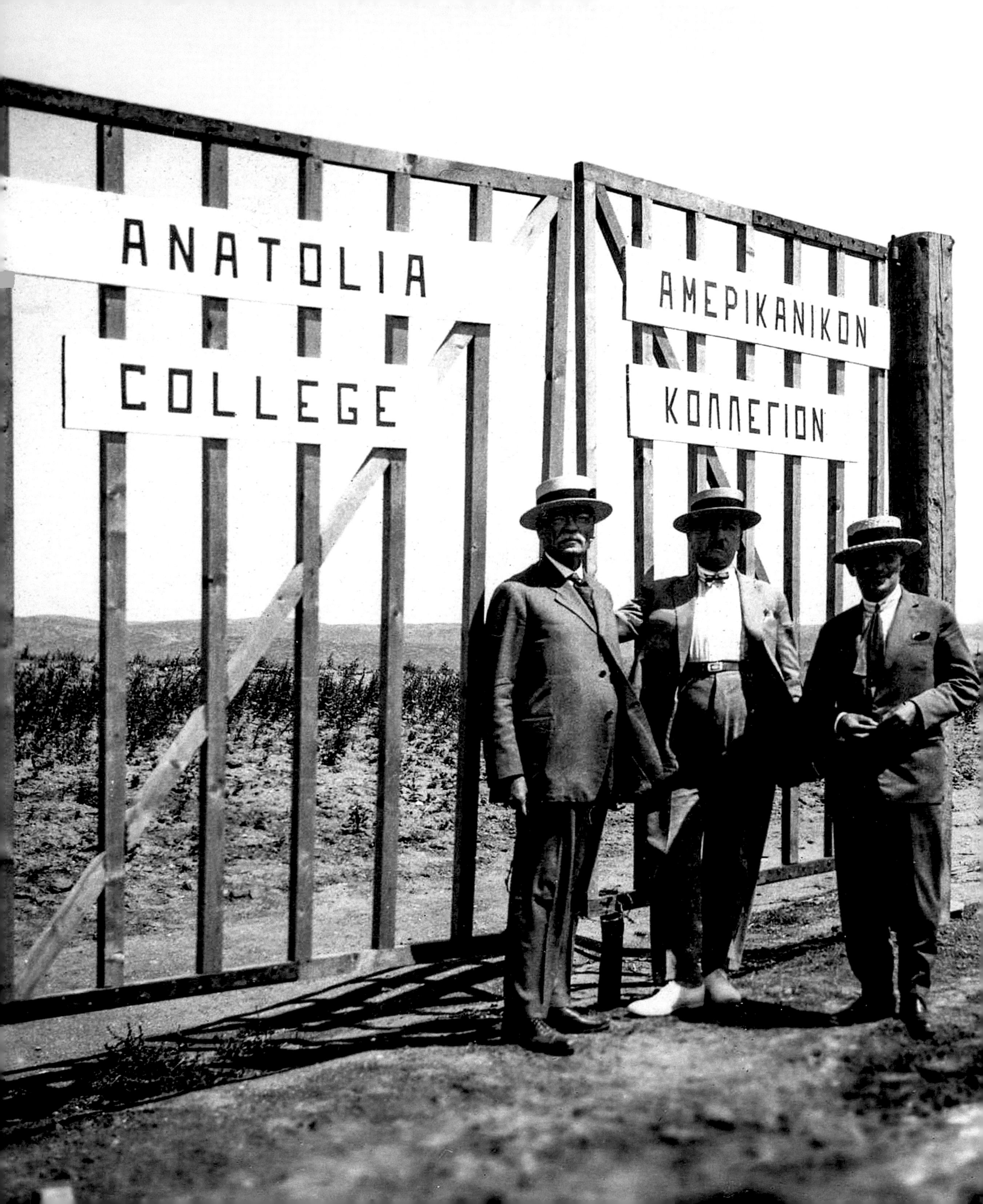
ANATOLIA
COLLEGE
ΑΜΕΡΙΚΑΝΙΚΟΝ
ΚΟΛΛΕΓΙΟΝ

AMERICAN COLLEGE, SALONICA, GREECE.
CONTINUING ANATOLIA COLLEGE

GEORGE E. WHITE, PRESIDENT OF THE COLLEGE

5D Anatolia College

Anatolia College was founded at the Merzifon (Marsovan) Seminary in 1886, based upon liberal arts ideals and principles of Christian education, emphasizing the humanities, humanistic values, and generous service to society. In 1923–1924, under the presidency of George E. White (1861–1946), Anatolia College relocated to Thessaloniki, its purpose being to better the lives of refugees and other impoverished young men through education. The school was first housed in an abandoned casino in the Charilaou area, where makeshift buildings functioned as dormitories for student boarders and staff: there was a dining hall, a special bathing area, and a large infirmary. In the vicinity open spaces were rented for students' sports, races, and intercollegiate championships. The student body consisted mostly of refugee children, including 14 former students from Merzifon. More than half of the students were orphans, many of them Armenians and Greeks. Students earned part of their expenses through employment: gardening, building maintenance, minor construction, crafting furniture in the carpentry shop, and serving meals in the dining hall.

The school effectively offered a non-sectarian, secular education that filled the needs of the Greek state and enjoyed the support of Bishop Gennadios in Thessaloniki and of Archbishop Athenagoras of the Greek Orthodox Archdiocese of America. While President White was mounting a successful fundraising campaign in the U.S. in the 1920s, the school was ably led by Dean Carl Compton, a "born educator" who taught by example in the classroom and on the sports fields, especially on the basketball court.

A significant development was the incorporation of the Mission School for Girls in Thessaloniki into Anatolia College in 1927. In 1934 the school moved to a newly constructed campus above the city, near the village of Pylea, on the lower slopes of Mt. Hortiatis, where it is still in operation.

M.G.

Opposite: President George E. White (left) at the gate of the new campus of Anatolia College on the current site between Pylea and Panorama, 1928.

Central building of Anatolia College in an abandoned casino in the Charilaou area of Thessaloniki, ca. 1925.

(Anatolia College Archives and Special Collections)

"Victory Day" and "Champions" pages from *The Anatolian* yearbook, 1929.

High jump during field day at Anatolia College, ca. 1926.

(Anatolia College Archives and Special Collections)

Girls class of 1928. (Anatolia College Archives and Special Collections)

Report for the annual meeting of the American College of Thessaloniki (Anatolia), 1926. (Near East Mission in Turkey, retrieved from: http://archives.saltresearch.org/handle/123456789/46666)

AMERICAN COLLEGE, SALONICA, GREECE.

CONTINUING ANATOLIA COLLEGE

GEORGE E. WHITE, PRESIDENT OF THE COLLEGE

ANNUAL MEETING - 1926.

The academic year 1925-1926 has brought a good deal to the American College at Salonica, continuing Anatolia College, for which we are grateful. The students enrolled numbered 170, of whom 5 were Albanian, 56 Armenian and 109 Greek. The limit of enrollment was strictly set for the limited facilities we are able to provide as yet, after the loss of our entire material plant and equipment in 1921. 130 students are already enrolled for entry next September, when we hope to provide for a total of 200.

The officers of administration and instruction numbered 19, of whom 10 were full-time teachers, the others being part-time teachers or occuppied with administrative duties

The YMCA of Thessaloniki operated from 1921 to 1924 in a two-story rented building at 19 Evzonon Street. (Kautz Family YMCA Archives, University of Minnesota Libraries)

5E The YMCA

The aim of the Young Men's Christian Association (YMCA) is to put Christian values into practice by developing a healthy "body, mind, and spirit," especially in youth. Owing to its Protestant penchant, it had not been permitted to operate in "Old Greece," but, in 1918, with the approval of Greek prime minister Eleftherios Venizelos, Americans Harvey Henderson and Richard Boardman of the International YMCA were allowed to develop wartime programs for Greek soldiers known as the "Soldiers' Huts." These offered canteen services, athletic and other physical recreation, cinemas, theatrical exhibitions, circulating libraries, lecture courses, lessons in Greek for illiterate soldiers, and religious and moral lectures.

The YMCA of Thessaloniki was founded in 1921 and the YMCA of Athens in 1923, both with support from locals and the Orthodox Church.

The YMCA had an active presence in refugee settlements such as Kokkinia and Nikaia in Piraeus and Kalamaria in Thessaloniki. Moreover, the Thessaloniki branch was especially effective in providing a variety of services to impoverished youth that were financed jointly by the central government, the municipality (which provided a prime building site), and with support from America. Under the energetic leadership of Ulius Amoss (1895–1961) and Herbert Parker Lansdale Jr. (1898–1988), the impressive YMCA building was inaugurated in 1928 in the center of Thessaloniki. It then housed the largest indoor basketball court in the Balkans.

In 1925 the YMCA established the oldest continuously operating summer camp in Greece, on Mount Pelion.

M.G.

Greek soldiers queuing at a "Soldiers' Hut" in Thessaloniki. (Retrieved from: www.searchculture.gr/aggregator/edm/Ymca/000075-11739_916)

The first basketball team of the Thessaloniki YMCA with the American Lewis Riess (right) and Symeon Mavroskoufis (left), head of physical education, 1926. (Retrieved from: www.searchculture.gr/aggregator/edm/Ymca/000075-11739_2542)

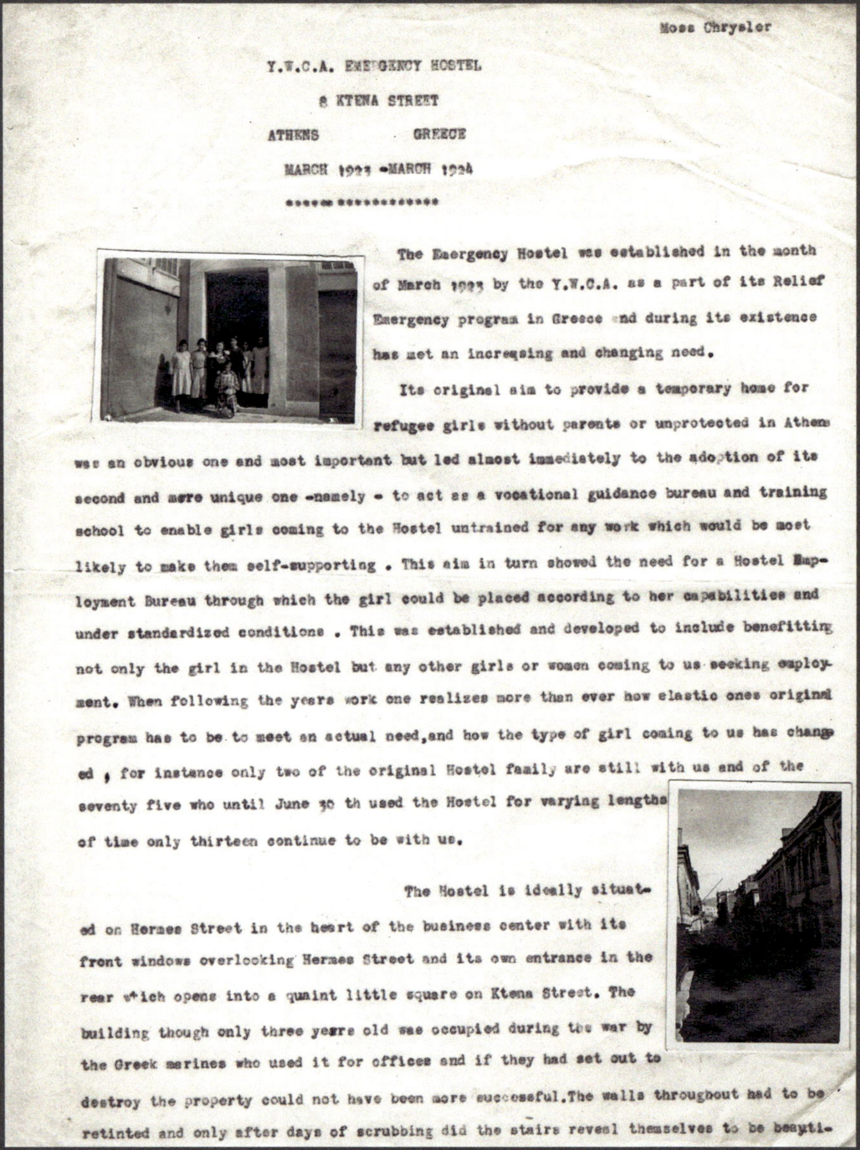

Moss Chrysler

Y.W.C.A. EMERGENCY HOSTEL

8 KTENA STREET

ATHENS GREECE

MARCH 1923 -MARCH 1924

****** ************

The Emergency Hostel was established in the month of March 1923 by the Y.W.C.A. as a part of its Relief Emergency program in Greece and during its existence has met an increasing and changing need.

Its original aim to provide a temporary home for refugee girls without parents or unprotected in Athens was an obvious one and most important but led almost immediately to the adoption of its second and more unique one -namely - to act as a vocational guidance bureau and training school to enable girls coming to the Hostel untrained for any work which would be most likely to make them self-supporting . This aim in turn showed the need for a Hostel Employment Bureau through which the girl could be placed according to her capabilities and under standardized conditions . This was established and developed to include benefitting not only the girl in the Hostel but any other girls or women coming to us seeking employment. When following the years work one realizes more than ever how elastic ones original program has to be to meet an actual need,and how the type of girl coming to us has changed , for instance only two of the original Hostel family are still with us and of the seventy five who until June 30 th used the Hostel for varying lengths of time only thirteen continue to be with us.

The Hostel is ideally situated on Hermes Street in the heart of the business center with its front windows overlooking Hermes Street and its own entrance in the rear which opens into a quaint little square on Ktena Street. The building though only three years old was occupied during the war by the Greek marines who used it for offices and if they had set out to destroy the property could not have been more successful.The walls throughout had to be retinted and only after days of scrubbing did the stairs reveal themselves to be beauti-

Theatrical performances at the Thessaloniki YMCA camp on Mount Pelion, 1928. (Retrieved from: www.searchculture.gr/aggregator/edm/Ymca/000075-11739_3284)

Report of the hostel of the Young Women's Christian Association (YWCA) in Athens for the period 1923–1924. Located at 8 Ktena Street, the hostel accommodated 62 orphan girls and young women who lived in Athens unescorted. (ASCSA Archives, Bert H. Hill Papers)

The YMCA Palace in Thessaloniki under construction, 1928. (Photo Liontas-Mavridis, Thessaloniki YMCA Archives, retrieved from: https://www.searchculture.gr/aggregator/edm/Ymca/000075-11739_2625)

Foundation of the YMCA Palace in Thessaloniki, March 2, 1924. In the front row (from left to right): Alexandros Michaelidis, General Alexandros Othonaios, Henry Morgenthau, John Mott, Mikes Mavrogordatos. (Kautz Family YMCA Archives, University of Minnesota Libraries)

First annual ball of the St. Constantine and Helen Greek Orthodox Community, Hotel Raleigh, Washington, D.C., December 8, 1921. Joannes Gennadius and his wife Florence are in the first row (fifth and sixth from left). (ASCSA, Gennadius Library, Joannes Gennadius Scrapbook)

6

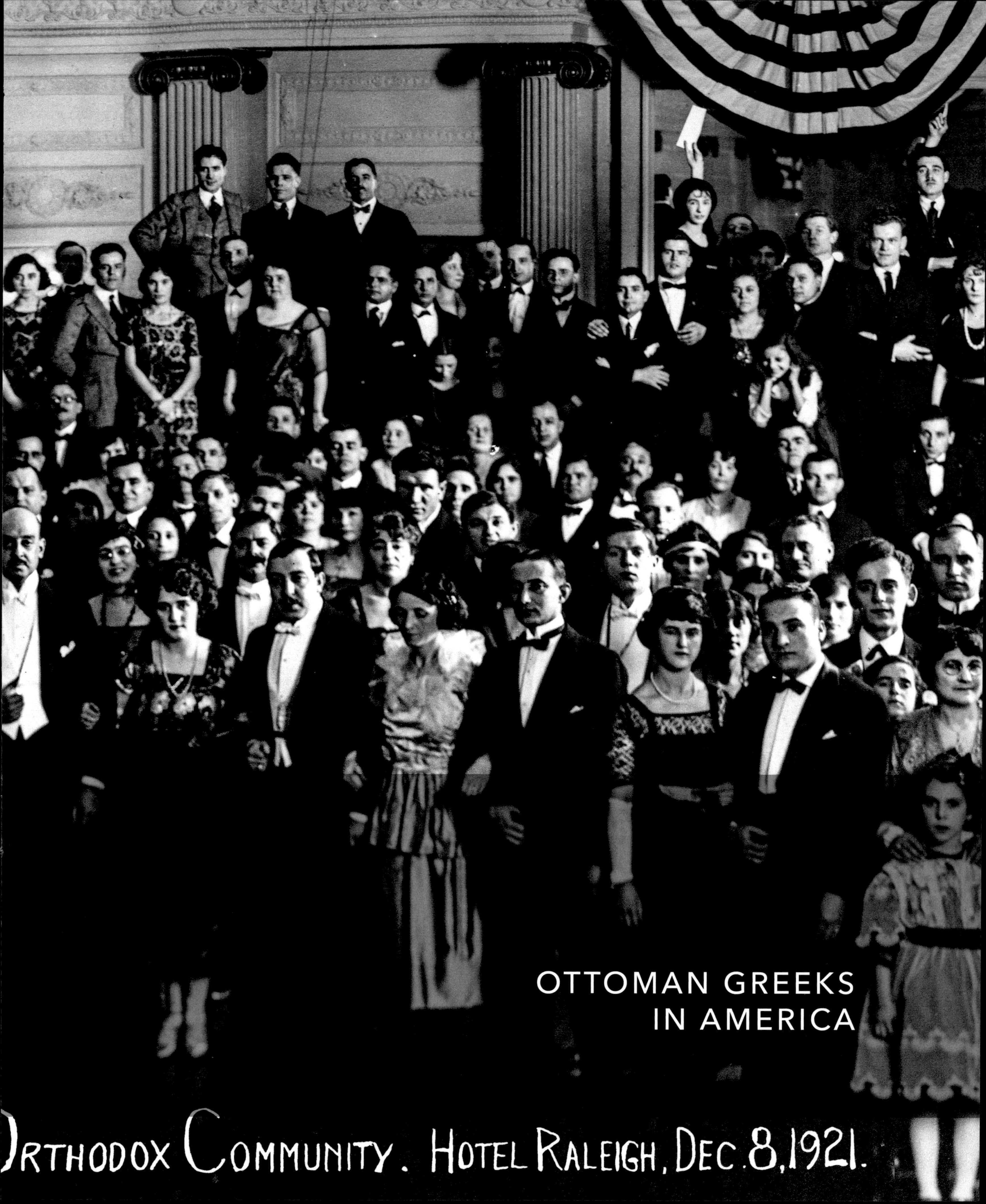

OTTOMAN GREEKS IN AMERICA

JAMES L. BARTON
CHAIRMAN
JOHN H. FINLEY
VICE-CHAIRMAN
CHARLES V. VICKREY
GENERAL SECRETARY
CLEVELAND H. DODGE
TREASURER
FRANK L. POLK
GENERAL COUNCIL

J. P. XENIDES
SEC. GREEK DEPT.

NEAR EAST RELIEF

INCORPORATED BY ACT OF CONGRESS
(FORMERLY AMERICAN COMMITTEE FOR ARMENIAN AND SYRIAN RELIEF)

CABLE ADDRESS NEAREAST — NEAR EAST RELIEF — TELEPHONE: ASHLAND 7480

151 FIFTH AVENUE
NEW YORK

EXECUTIVE COMMITTEE
EDWIN BULKLEY, CHR.
JAMES L. BARTON
CLEVELAND H. DODGE
ABRAM I. ELKUS
HAROLD A. HATCH
WILLIAM B. MILLAR
HENRY MORGENTHAU
GEORGE A. PLIMPTON
WALTER GEORGE SMITH
CHARLES V. VICKREY
STANLEY WHITE

Χριστούγεννα, 1921

Πρὸς τὸν Ἑλληνισμὸν τῆς Ἀμερικῆς.

Ἀγαπητοὶ φίλοι:

Ἡ ταλαίπωρος Ἀνατολὴ εἰσέτι εὑρίσκεται εἰς τραγικὴν ἐμπόλεμον κατάστασιν καὶ οἱ ἐκεῖ χριστιανικοὶ πληθυσμοί, ἄνδρες, γυναῖκες καὶ παιδία, ὑφίστανται τρομερὰς σπαραξικαρδίους συμφοράς. Ὅσοι δὲν ἔπεσον θύματα σφαγῶν καὶ θανατώσεων, ἐξωρίσθησαν εἰς τὰ ἐνδότερα τῆς Μικρᾶς Ἀσίας, ὅπου ἀποθνήσκουν ἀπὸ πεῖναν, ἀσθενείας, κακώσεις καὶ ἐξαντλήσεις. Ὅσοι δὲ μένουν εἰσέτι εἰς τὰς ἑστίας των—ἐν γένει μόνον γυναικόπαιδα—ὑποφέρουν τὰ πάνδεινα, ἐστερημένοι ὅλων τῶν μέσων τῆς συντηρήσεως των.

Ὅλα δὲ αὐτὰ ἔρχονται ἐπιπροσθέτως εἰς τὰς χιλιάδας τῶν ὀρφανῶν καὶ ἄλλων θυμάτων τῶν προηγουμένων ἐτῶν τοῦ πολέμου, τὰ ὁποῖα ἤδη εὑρίσκονται εἰς τὰ ὀρφανοτροφεῖα, συσσίτια καὶ νοσοκομεία τῆς Ἐπιτροπῆς τῆς Περιθάλψεως ἐν τῇ Ἐγγὺς Ἀνατολῇ.

Θαρροῦντες ἐπὶ τῆς καλῶς ἐγνωσμένης γενναιοδωρίας καὶ φιλανθρωπίας τῶν Ἑλλήνων τῆς Ἀμερικῆς, ἰδιαιτέρως δὲ ἐκτιμῶντες μεγάλως τὴν μέχρι τοῦδε σπουδαίαν συμβολὴν αὐτῶν εἰς τὸ ἔργον τῆς Περιθάλψεως, ζητοῦμεν ἅπαξ ἔτι τὴν βοήθειάν σας εἰς τὰς σημερινὰς κρισίμους περιστάσεις ὁπότε αἱ ἀνάγκαι εἶνε εἴπερ ποτε ἐπείγουσαι.

Ἐνῶ λοιπὸν ἑτοιμάζεσθε νὰ ἑορτάσητε μετὰ τῶν ἐδῶ προσφιλῶν σας τὰ Χριστούγενα καὶ τὸ Νέον Ἔτος ἐν εἰρήνῃ, ἀσφαλείᾳ καὶ χαρᾷ, ἐν τῇ ἐλευθέρᾳ ταύτῃ καὶ φιλοξένῳ Δημοκρατίᾳ, παρακαλεῖσθε νὰ ἐνθυμηθῆτε τοὺς δυστυχεῖς ἀδελφούς μας τοὺς ἀναστενάζοντας μακρὰν τῶν ἑστιῶν των ἐν ἐξορίᾳ, τὰ ἀθῶα ὀρφανά μας, καὶ τὰς χιλιάδας χιλιάδων ἄλλων θυμάτων τὰ ὁποῖα περιπλανῶνται τῇδε κακεῖσε πεινασμένα, γυμνὰ καὶ ἄστεγα. Ἂς ἠχήσουν εἰς τὰ ὦτα σας ἡ φωνὴ τῶν βρεφῶν, αἱ οἰμωγαὶ τῶν μητέρων καὶ οἱ ὀδυρμοὶ ὅλων τῶν ταλαιπώρων ἀδελφῶν μας. Ὅλοι αὐτοὶ ζητοῦν βοήθειαν καὶ προστασίαν. Ἂν δὲν σπεύσωμεν ἀμέσως εἰς βοήθειάν των κινδυνεύουν ὅλοι νὰ καταστραφοῦν.

"SAVE A LIFE"

Στείλατε παρακαλοῦμεν τὰ ὑπὲρ αὐτῶν δῶρά σας, μὲ συνάλλαγμα, ταχυδρομικὴν ἐπιταγήν, ἢ ὁποιονδήποτε ἄλλο μέσον τῆς εὐκολίας σας, ἐπ' ὀνόματι τῆς Near East Relief,

151 Fifth Avenue, New York.

Διὰ τὴν Near East Relief

J. Gennadius

On behalf of the NER, Greek diplomat Joannes Gennadius composed in Greek an appeal letter to the Greeks in America to support the thousands of orphans being cared for by the organization, Christmas 1921. (ASCSA Archives, Joannes Gennadius Papers)

6A Greek Americans and Ottoman Greek Migrants in the U.S.

A new influx of Orthodox migrants from the Ottoman Empire was added to the mass transatlantic migration of Greek workers that had begun in 1890. U.S. immigration authorities on Ellis Island sometimes labeled them as "Ottoman Greeks."

The turbulence caused by war, natural disasters, and socioeconomic instability contributed to both voluntary and forced migration of approximately 100,000 Ottoman Greek migrants in the first quarter of the 20th century. Some settled in migrant enclaves while others followed opportunities presented by the job market. Most found employment as unskilled laborers in confectionaries, flower shops, restaurants, factories, railroads, mines, and in construction and service industries.

Until 1922, many immigrants maintained strong ties with their communities in the Ottoman Empire and made impactful monetary contributions to their families through the nascent Greek Orthodox Church in America, which acted as a community-building institution, or through Greek and Ottoman Greek mutual aid organizations. The exchange of populations permanently severed those ties and left Ottoman Greek migrants with limited choices: live permanently in the U.S. or in the Kingdom of Greece. The Immigration Act of 1924 limited the number of immigrants allowed entry into the U.S. by imposing a national origins quota.

Many philanthropic activities took place at the prestigious Palm Gardens in Manhattan. The fundraising dance of the Pan-Ionian Association of America (1920) kicked off a successful fundraising drive in support of the St. Charalambos Hospital of Smyrna. (Ottoman Greeks of the U.S. Digital History Project, University of Florida)

This exhibition traces the establishment and philanthropic activity between 1915 and 1922 of 11 Ottoman Greek organizations in respect to their associated communities in the Ottoman Empire and in the Kingdom of Greece. Located in Los Angeles, New York City, Somerville, Massachusetts, and Tacoma, Washington, these organizations bonded their members in communities in America, while contributing to the preservation of their homelands in the Ottoman Empire. Similar activities sponsored by Greek immigrants from Greece point out a rift in priorities between those from "Old Greece" and the Ottoman Greeks, owing to their different origins and linguistic backgrounds.

Descendants of Ottoman Greek immigrants recall a total of 12 language categories used at home by their grandparents. The most common was demotic Greek with Turkish words used sparingly. Some spoke Turkish and used English sparingly. Other languages included Arvanitika, Arabic, Mytilenian/West Anatolian Greek, Pontic, French, Katharevousa Greek, Greeklish, Polish, and Lazika.

Y.T.

OAGAPITICOS
TIS VOSCOPOULAS

GIVEN BY THE
HELLENIC DRAMATIC AND MUSICAL
SOCIETY

FOR THE BENEFIT OF THE WOUNDED
SOLDIERS IN GREECE

CARROLL HALL : 924 G STREET N. W.

SUNDAY, DECEMBER 18, 1921

PRICE $1.00 INCLUDING WAR TAX

7

Opposite: Ticket for a fundraising performance of the Greek bucolic romance "The Lover of the Shepherdess," which attracted many Greek Americans when staged for the benefit of the wounded soldiers of Greece at Carrol Hall in Washington, D.C., December 20, 1921. (ASCSA, Gennadius Library,Joannes Gennadius Scrapbook)

The Greek American newspaper *National Herald* announced the results of the fundraising campaign to help the refugees on September 5, 1923. The money collected was matched by the Near East Relief; nearly $440,000 was sent to Athens within a year. (Digital repository of the *National Herald*)

ΕΝ ΟΝΟΜΑΤΙ ΤΗΣ ΕΘΝΙΚΗΣ ΤΙΜΗΣ

ΒΟΗΘΗΣΑΤΕ

ΤΑ ΟΡΦΑΝΑ ΤΗΣ ΠΑΤΡΙΔΟΣ ΣΑΣ

Κόπτετε κάθε μῆνα ὅλοι ἀνὰ ἓν δολλάριον ἀπὸ τὰ περιττά σας ἔξοδα καὶ στέλλετέ το εἰς τὸν Ἔρανον ὑπὲρ τῶν θυμάτων τῆς καταστροφῆς.

Η ΚΑΤΑΣΤΑΣΙΣ ΤΟΥ ΕΡΑΝΟΥ

Αἱ μέχρι σήμερον εἰσφοραὶ

$219.725.39

Εἰσφοραὶ Αὐγούστου .... Δολλ. 540.63

Σύνολον ἀποστολῶν ὑπὲρ τῶν Ἑλλήνων προσφύγων εἰς Ἀθήνας, Κωνσταντινούποιν καὶ Χαλέπιον, διπλασιαζομένων ὑπὸ τῆς NEAR EAST RELIEF:

$423.261.84

Ὑπόλοιπον εἰς χεῖράς μας μέχρι σήμερον:

$8.176.47

ΝΕΟΙ ΕΡΑΝΟΙ ὑπὲρ τῶν θυμάτων τῆς Μικρασιατικῆς καταστροφῆς προερχόμενοι ἀπὸ τὰς ἑξῆς παροικίας:

WATERTOWN, MASS.

Συνεχίζουν τὰς ἀποστολάς των.— Νέον ἔμβασμα ἐκ δολλαρίων 106.

Watertown, 27 Ἰουλίου.

Ἀξιότιμε Κύριε Διευθυντὰ τοῦ «Ἐθνικοῦ Κήρυκος»

Ἐσωκλείστως εὑρίσκετε ταχυδρο- τῆς παροικίας μας, κατ' ἀπαίτησιν τῶν μελῶν αὐτοῦ ὅπως σταλοῦν ὑπὲρ τοῦ ἄνω σκοποῦ.

Δημοσιεύσατε, παρακαλοῦμεν, καὶ τὰ ἔσοδα καὶ ἔξοδα, ἅτινα εἶναι ὡς ἑξῆς.

ΕΣΟΔΑ.—Ἀπὸ δωρεὰς καὶ μηνιαίας συνδρομὰς δολλ. 214.50.

ΕΞΟΔΑ.—Ἀναγνώρισις Τμήματος εἰς Κέντρον δολλ. 50, ἐνοίκιον αἰθούσης συνελεύσεων δολ. 10, εἰς εἰσπράκτορα 7.50. Τὸ ὅλον δολλ. 67.50.

Ντζοιμάνης 5, Δημήτριος Τσιγγάρης 5, Γεώργιος Κέλης 3, Σωτήριος Σάφης 2.50, Καλιφόρνια Φρούτ Στόρ 2.50, Δημήτριος Κόσκαλης 3, Νικόλαος Ντζοιμάνης 2, Στέφανος Κυριδάκης 2, Ἰωάννης Παπαντέλης 5, Ἀντώνιος Κυπριδάκης 1, Κωνσταντῖνος Λεφάκης ἢ Φραγκογιάννης 3, Δημήτριος Τριπολίτης 1.

Ὁ κ. Ἐυ. Βάρπας, ἐκ Palisade τοῦ Κολοράδου, στέλλει δολλ. 3.

Εἷς ἀνώνυμος ἐκ Dover, N. H. καίτοι ἐλησμόνησε τὸ ὄνομά του δὲν ἐλησμόνησε καὶ τοὺς ἀδελφούς του. Στέλλει δολλ. 2 εἰς τὸν ἔρανον.

ΒΛΑΔΙΒΟΣΤΟΚ, ΣΙΒΗΡΙΑΣ.

Στέλλει δολλ. 50 ἀπὸ τὰς ἐσχατιὰς τοῦ Κόσμου, εἰς ἀνακούφισιν τῶν ἀναξιοπαθούντων ἀδελφῶν μας.

ΒΛΑΔΙΒΟΣΤΟΚ, 14 Ἰουλίου.

Ἀξιότιμε Κύριε Διευθυντά,

Ἐσωκλείστως ἐν τῇ παρούσῃ μου εὑρίσκετε ἐπιταγὴν εἰς διαταγήν σας διὰ δολλ. 55, ἐκ τῶν ὁποίων τὰ μὲν πέντε δολλάρια παρακαλῶ νὰ δώσητε εἰς τὸ Τμῆμα τῶν συνδρομῶν τῆς ἐφημερίδος σας, ὁμοῦ μετὰ τοῦ ἐπισυνημμένου δελτίου, πρὸς ἀνανέωσιν τῆς συνδρομῆς μου διὰ 6 μῆνας, τὰ δὲ 50 δολλάρια, παρακαλῶ νὰ δοθῶσιν εἰς τὸν ὑπὲρ τῶν προσφύγων μας ἔρανόν σας, ὡς ἐλαχίστην ἐκ μέρους μου προσφορὰν ὑπὲρ τῶν δυστυχῶν αὐτῶν ἀνθρώπων. Ἐὰν ἐν τῷ ὀργανισμῷ τοῦ ἐράνου ὑπάρχῃ ἰδιαίτερον ταμεῖον διὰ τοὺς ἐκ Πόντου πρόσφυγας, δώσατε παρακαλῶ τὴν συνεισφοράν μου εἰς τὸ Ταμεῖον αὐτό, εἰδ' ἄλλως διαθέσατέ το ὅπως κρίνετε καλλίτερον.

Δράττομαι δὲ τῆς περιστάσεως ὅπως ὅπως ἐκφράσω ὑμῖν τὰ συγχαρητήριά μου ἐπὶ τῷ πατριωτικῷ ἔργῳ τοῦ ὑ-

Annual picnic of the Los Angeles Benevolent Association of the Marmarians, whose members came from the village of Afthoni in Marmara. Elysian Park, Los Angeles, date unknown. (Ottoman Greeks of the U.S. Digital History Project, University of Florida)

General catalogue of Greek, Turkish, and Albanian records of the RCA Victor Records company. (Personal collection of Christopher C. King)

6B The Music of Ottoman Greek Migrants in America

With modest incomes, Greeks and Armenians from Asia Minor were able to satisfy their hunger for music of their homelands by listening to live artists in "Oriental clubs" and in urban tavernas in the Greektowns of major cities. Wealthier immigrants purchased the recently mass-produced phonograph player, or "talking machine," along with 78-rpm records of *demotika*, *rembetiko*, and popular music in their own language.

How Asia Minor Music Was Captured on 78-Rpm Records in America

It was only in the late teens and early 1920s that the major recording companies (Columbia and Victor, later RCA Victor), decided to target recently arrived immigrant populations—such as Greeks from Asia Minor—and to give them recordings in their local styles and language. Greek folk music had been recorded in Istanbul, Izmir, Thessaloniki, and Athens by European companies such as UK Gramophone and His Master's Voice, but was limited in tastes. Most Asia Minor Greeks in the early 1920s wanted to hear music from their regions.

In the early 1920s the major phonograph companies in America sought out specific Greek artists and recorded them in their studios, mainly in New York City and Chicago, but occasionally on the West Coast, probably as a response to the influx of Asia Minor migrants. Greek and Greek-American instrumentalists and singers recorded an extremely diverse repertoire from mainland Greece, the Aegean Islands, and Asia Minor. By 1941, a few thousand recordings of Greek music had been issued in America by the diaspora artists; Greek-language records eventually constituted more than a sixth of the total sales of domestic records in the U.S.! Not only did the major American labels inadvertently preserve Greek regional styles but they also promoted the careers of several singers and musicians who recorded extensively.

Asia Minor immigrants had a tremendous musical influence in America, and some of the musicians created their own Greek-language record labels focusing on regional music. Kyriaki Yiortzi Antonopoulou (Madame Koula) created the Panhellenion Phonograph Record Company in 1919 in New York City after she recorded several disks for Columbia Records. And, between 1922 and 1923, George Dimitrios Grechis established the Greek Record Company in Chicago. Both labels featured exceptional Asia Minor musicians and an extensive repertoire in their catalogues, which were promoted in Greek-language American newspapers. A broad panorama of regional styles were preserved within the grooves of these shellac records.

The Artists and the Legacy

Many Asia Minor musicians had their first and only opportunity to record in America. Gus Dussas, a refugee from Tripoli, Anatolia, in the 1930s recorded in Chicago his unique introspective *zeibekiko*, a form of guitar and vocal *rembetiko* that did not take root in the contemporary Greek mainland. Similarly, Leonidas Smyrneos recorded several rare dance tunes from his native Izmir in 1927. The massive surge of Asia Minor migrants to the U.S. propelled the career of Tetos Demetriades as he became an important artist and repertoire man for RCA Victor and Orthophonic Records. Musicians such as Alexis Zoumbas, Marika Papagika, Achilles Poulos, and George Katsaros enjoyed long recording careers in America because they had mastered the Asia Minor songbook.

C.C.K.

Opposite: The ensemble of Konstantinos N. Kereakoglou (cornet, far left) and Michalis Kereakoglou (valve trombone, far right), originally from the village of Kapi, Lesvos, in Lynn, Massachusetts, ca. 1922. (Used by permission of the family of Konstantinos N. Kereakoglou)

ΔΙΣΚΟΙ 12 ΙΝΤΣΩΝ ΚΟΥΛΑΣ

8008 'Αλάμπεης (Εὐζωνικό μπεράτι).—Τσάμικος 'Ηπειρο-Μακεδονίας, ...$1.25
8007 Λιασκοβίτικος Τσάμικος. 'Ηπειρώτικο μοιρολόϊ 1.25
8027 Συρτό Χανιώτικο Σούστα 'Ηρακλειώτικη 1.25
8028 Κρητικό νυφιάτικο Πεντοζάλη 1.25
215 Στ' 'Αναπλιού τὸ Παλαμίδι (τσάμικο). Μάνα μιὰ κόρ' ἀγάπησα, συρτό. $1.25
216 'Αγαπῶ ἕνα χελιδόνι (τσάμικο). Μέσ' στὴν 'Αγιὰ Παρασκευή,— (συρτό) 1.25
217 Διαμαντούλα (κλέφτικο). Στὴν "Αδη θὰ κατέβω (συρτό).... 1.25
202 Πέσ' μου τί κακὸ τί ἀπονιά 'Ο Ψευτόκοσμος 1.25
8024 Κουτσαβάκι (ὑπὸ Κούλας) Βρὲ βλαμάκη, κάνε πέρα (ζεϊμ.) 1.25
8020 Ποιὰ σκύλλα μάνα (Κλέφτικο). Λαρίσσα (Κλέφτικο) $1.25
8023 Νυφιάτικο (Συρτό) Σήμερα γάμος γίνεται (συρτό) . 1.25
8025 Μηχανικὸς (χορὸς μόν. ὄργανα) Πολίτικο (συρτὸ μόνον ὄργανα). 1.25
8026 'Ελενάκ (Καρσιλαμὰς ὑπὸ Κούλας). Μπάλος φὰ ματζόρε (Κούλας) 1.25
206 'Ενύχτωσε ποιόνε θὰ 'δῶ (κλέφτικο). "Οταν σὲ βλέπω στὸ χορό, συρτό, 1.25
8000 Καλαματιανὸ (μόνον ὄργανα). Στὰ Σάλωνα (μόνον ὄργανα) 1.25
8001 Τριανταφυλλιὰ (μόνον ὄργανα). Μπαρατινὸ (μόνον ὄργανα) 1.25
8002 Κόδω μιὰ κλάρα (Τσάμικο). Κυρὰ Βαγγελιὼ (συρτό) 1.25
8003 'Εττιά (Τσάμικο, μόνον ὄργα). Βασίλω (συρτό). 1.25
8004 Παιδιάμ' σὰν θέλετε λεβέντιά Στῆς γαλανῆς τὸ φόρεμα 1.25
8005 Στῆς 'Αρκαδιάς τὸ Διάσελο. Τζάνεμ, ποταμέ μου, ... 1.25
8006 'Αετὸς (Τσάμικο). Στὴν κεντημένη σου ποδιά 1.25
8010 Διαμάντω (Τσάμικο). Παρόρι (ὑπὸ Κούλας) 1.25
8012 Παιδιά γιατί 'στε ἀνάλαγα Περιβόλι εἶχα πάπια μ' 1.25
8014 'Ο Λιούλιος (Τσάμικο). 'Εσοῦτει εἶναι βάσανα 1.25
8015 Τρία πουλάκια (Κλέφτικο). Λεμονάκι μυρωδάτο 1.25
8016 Κάνουν ν' ἀνθίσουν τὰ κλαριά. Κόρη μαλαματένια μου 1.25
8017 Κατσαντώνης (Κλέφτικο). 'Ο Καπετὰν Βάρδας 1.25
8918 Δκοσούλα (Κλέφτικο) Λάμπει ὁ ἥλιος στὰ βουνά 1.25
205 Κίνησα ὁ μαῦρος, κίνησα (Κλέφτικο). Παίρνω τὰ ζαχαράκια μου......... 1.25
207 'Οδυσσεὺς 'Ανδροῦτσος (Κλέφτικο). Σπάσε, γλυκειὰ φλογέρα 1.25
210 Κακὸ Ζακόνι (Κλέφτικο). Δώδεκα χρόνια φυλακή 1.25
212 Κιτρολεμονιὰ (Τσάμικο) Μοῦ παρήγγειλε τ' ἀηδόνι 1.25
213 Κότα μου (συρτὸ ὑπὸ Κούλας). 'Ο Γιώργης ὁ Μαραθιανὸς....... 1.25
5051 'Ο Μάγκας (ὑπὸ Κούλας). "Ολοι ο[illegible]ζο μὲ φωνάζουν, Κούλα 1.25
214 'Ανάθεμά σε, ξενητειά. Μωρὴ κακὴ γειτόνισσα. τσάμικο 1.25
222 Στὸ εἶπα, περδικοῦλά μου. Οὔλα τ[illegible] πουλάκια (συρτό) 1.25
250 Βιολέττα (Μαζοῦρκα). 'Ερωτευμένο πουλί, φὸξ τρότ, .. 1.25
251 Χορὸς 'Οριεντάλ ('Ισπανικός). Φρεμίτυ Ντ' ἀμὸρ (βάλς) 1.25
5050 'Η νέα Χάϊδω (Κούλας) 'Η 'Ατσιγγάνα (Κούλας) 1.25

ΔΙΣΚΟΙ 10 ΙΝΤΣΩΝ ΚΟΥΛΑΣ

ΔΙΣΚΟΙ ΟΡΦΕΟΜ ΚΩΝ)ΠΟΛΕΩΣ

100 Χιτζάζ Γκαζέλ μὲ ζουρνά Ούσσακ Γκαζέλ (μανές) $1.00
101 Ξύπνα, ξύπνα, γλυκειά μου παρθένα. Γιὰφ Γιοῦφ 1.00
104 Τσιφτὲ Τέλλ (ζουρνάς) Γαλατά μανὲς (Κων)πόλεως) ... 1.00

ΑΘΗΝΑ·Ι·ΚΑ ΑΣΜΑΤΑ

305 'Αραχνιασμένο μνῆμα Οἱ ξενύχτηδες 1.00
306 Σ' ὁρκίζομαι Θέλω νὰ ἰδῶ τὸν Πάπα 1.00
307 "Ελα (διῳδία). Σὲ ἀγαπῶ (διῳδία), ... 1.00
308 Μαζούρκα ὑπὸ ὀρχήστρας. Σοτὶς ὑπὸ ὀρχήστρας 1.00
309 Κική Συνταγματάρχου Ψηλὰ στὸ μέτωπο 1.00
5024 Σερενάδα Σὶρ Διονύσιου (Κανάκη) "Αχ Μαρὶ (Κανάκη) 1.00
7000 Τὸν κόσμον ἔχω βαρεθῆ. Καμαριέρα $1.00
7001 "Οπως τ' ἀστέρι τὴ χαραυγή. Φουντα βράκα.......... 1.00
7002 Παραμύθι Νεράϊδας. Σφίξε με. 1.00
7003 Μακρὰν κι' ἂν εἶσαι. Μαργαρίτα 1.00
7004 'Η ἄπονος καρδιά. Στὰ ὡραῖά σου μαλλιά 1.00
7005 Τί ποθῶ. Τὸ Τσοπανόπουλο 1.00
7006 "Εχει καϋμοὺς ἡ θάλασσα. Μικρὴ ξανθή 1.00
7007 Τρελλή μου καστανή Προτιμένω 1.00
7.008 Λάμπει μέσ' στὸ γιαλό. Τὶκ - Τὰκ ἡ καρδιά μου 1.00
7009 'Η ὄλια σου ματιά, "Εχω ἕνα μάτι φλογερὸ 1.00
7010 Γιατί ὁπόταν σὲ κυττῶ (ὑπὸ Γ. Γεωργίου καὶ Μ. Θελετρίδου). Γιατί σὰν ἄστρο, γαλανή, ... 1.00

ΔΙΣΚΟΙ ΚΟΥΛΑΣ

5045 Νέος 'Αλὴ Πασσᾶς (Κούλας). 'Ωραία Μανιατοποῦλα Κούλας, 1.00
5047 Μπάρμπα Γιάννης (ζεϊμπέκ. Κούλας). 'Αλιπιάρη μὲ φωνάζουν, Κούλα, 1.00
5048 Ξύπνα καϋμένη 'Αναστασιά (Κούλας) Τ' ἔχεις καϋμένε Πλάτανε, ... 1.00
5049 'Εσεῖς πουλιὰ τοῦ κάμπου (Κούλας). Βασίλω Καλαματιανή, Κούλας, 1.00
4000 'Η Γκόλφω (ὑπὸ Κούλας), Τσοπανάκος ἤμουνα 1.00
4001 Τοῦ Κίτσου ἡ μάνα (Κλέφτικο), Παπαδιά)συρτό), ... 1.00
4002 Στῆς μαντζουράνας τὸν ἀνθὸ (Τσάμικο, ὑπὸ Γεώργη), Μιὰ Σμυρνιὰ στὸ παραθύρι, ... 1.00
4005 Νταβέλης (Τσάμικο). Τὸ παπάκι (συρτό). 1.00
4006 Γιουσοὺφ 'Αράπης (Τσάμικο) Λουλοῦδι τῆς Μονεμβασιάς ... 1.00
4007 Σ' ἀγαπῶ, Γαρουφαλιά μου. Νέα Τριανταφυλλιά 1.00
4008 'Ο Ταέλιος Κλέφτικο. Τώρα τὰ πουλιά 1.00
4009 'Η Νίνα (Χασάπικο). Ζεϊμπέκικο 'Αϊβαλιώτικο 1.00
4010 Ποιὰ μάννα ἔχει δυὸ παιδιά. 'Ο Γέρω Νότης (κλέφτικο) 1.00
4012 Χεζζάζ μανὲς (ὑπὸ Γεώργη). Βαστάτε, Τοῦρκοι, τ' ἄλογα 1.00
4013 'Η 'Αράχωβα (Τσάμικο). Παναγιώτισσα Λυγερή 1.00
4021 'Αρβανίτικο μοιρολόϊ (κλαρίνο). Μπεράτι χορὸς (κλαρίνο) 1.00
4022 Σιάτιστα χορὸς (κλαρίνο). Κάϊδα (κλαρίνο, Θ. Ζάκας), ... 1.00
4023 Κοζανίτικος χορὸς (κλαρίνο). Τσάμικο Μακεδονίας (κλαρίνο) 1.00
4024 'Ηπειρώτικος χορὸς (Μακεδόνας βιολί) Γιαννιώτικο μοιρολόϊ (Μακεδόνα 1.00
7015 Συγκαθιστὸς χορὸς (ὑπὸ Ζάκα). Χασάπικος χορὸς (ὑπὸ Ζάκα) .. 1.00
7016 Νυφιάτικος χορὸς (ὑπὸ Ζάκα). Βολιώτικος χορὸς (ὑπὸ Ζάκα) . 1.00
5005 Δυὸ ψαράκια μελανοῦρια. Μπάλος καὶ ἀμανὲς 1.00
5007 Τὸ λὲν οἱ κοῦκοι στὰ βουνά. Σήκω, Δημήτρω, κι' ἄλλαξε ... 1.00
5011 Κάτω στὸ γιαλό, (Χιώτικο). "Ολες ἡ πακαροῦνες 1.00
5020 Τὰ οὖλά σου (Ζεϊμπέκικο, Κούλας). Σαμιώτισσα 'Αθην. ἆσμα, Κούλας 1.00
5021 'Εγὼ τὸ πίνω, (νέον 'Αθηναϊκὸν ἆσμα). Στόμα μὲ στόμα, ν. 'Αθ. ἆσμα, .. 1.00
5022 'Εμβατήριον Βενιζέλου (Γ. Κανάκη) 'Εθνικὸς ὕμνος, (ὀρχ. καὶ ἆσμ.). 1.00
5023 Τοῦ 'Αητοῦ ὁ Γυιὸς (ὑπὸ Γ. Κανάκη). 'Η Σημαία μας, ... 1.00
5025 Ράστυ μανὲς (ὑπὸ Κούλας, μὲ ἀρμόνικα).—"Αχ, τί θὰ γεννῶ, τρελλοκόριτσο, (Κούλας μὲ ἀρμόνικα). 1.00
5026 Σαμπάχ, μανές, (Κούλας μὲ ἀρμόνικα Γγλυκειά μου Σπαρτιάτισσα (μὲ ἀρμόνικα) 1.00
5027 'Αρμενάκι, σοῦστα, (ὑπὸ Κούλας). Καροτσιέρης (Χασάπικο). 1.00
5028 Οὔλες ἡ δάφνες, τσάμικο, (ὑπὸ Κούλας Μαλάμω (συρτό) 1.00
5029 Στὰ Σάλωνα (νέον, ὑπὸ Κούλας). Φῶτα τὸ φεγγαράκι μου, Κούλας 1.00
5030 Μαυροζερούλα (Τσάμικο, ὑπὸ Κούλας, τῇ συνοδείᾳ 'Ελληνικῶν ὀργάνων).—Μπερατιανό, συρτό 1.00
5031 Μαργιόλικο, τσάμικο, (Κούλα). "Εβγα, ἥλιε, (Κούλας). 1.00
5032 Ψαράκι, (Χιώτικο συρτό, Κούλας). Μπάτε, κορίτσια, (Κούλας) ... 1.00
5033 'Η Βασιλ' ἀρχόντισσα (Κλέφτικο, ὑπὸ Κίτσου, τῇ συνοδείᾳ 'Ελλ. ὀργ). Μιὰ Βλάχα (Κούλας) 1.00
5034 Θεοδ. Γρίβας (Κλέφτικο, ὑπὸ Κούλας) Καπετὰν Ζάκας (κλαρίνο, Μακεδόνα, καὶ Κούλας) 1.00
5036 'Η Μαγιορή (Τσάμικο, Κούλας). Καλαματιανὸ (συρτό) 1.00
5938 Μπαίνω μέσ' στ' ἀμπέλι (συρτό, Κούλας).—'Αργίτικο, συρτό, (βιολί, κλαρίνο καὶ σαντοῦρι) 1.00
5039 Σαμιώτικο, νυφιάτικο συρτό (βιολί, κλαρίνο καὶ σαντοῦρι),—'Αμὰν 'Αμάν, Χιώτισσα, (ζεϊμπέκικο) 1.00
5041 Τζανταρμάς, ζεϊμπέκικο, (κορνέτα, βιολί, κλαρίνο καὶ σαντοῦρι).—Πιγγί, ζεϊμπέκικο, (κορνέτα, βιολί, κλαρίνο καὶ σαντοῦρι) .... .100
5043 'Αζιζιὲ συρτὸ (νησιώτικο). Ζεϊμπέκικο (Μικρασιάτικο βαρύ)1.00
5044 Μυτιληνιὸ Ζεϊμπέκικο. Τοῦ Κίτσου ἡ μάννα (συρτό) 1.00
6011 Κάτω στὸν κάμπο (Τσάμικο). "Ας πὰν νὰ δοῦν τὰ μάτια μου, ... 1.00
6016 Τζιοβαίρι ἡ χήρα (ἆσμα ὑπὸ Κούλας). Ματζόρε μανὲς (Κούλας) 1.00

ΔΙΣΚΟΙ ΤΟΥ ΚΑΡΑΓΚΙΟΖΗ

7021 Τζιώτικο Ραβαΐσι, μέρος Α', (κωμῳδία Λεονταρη).—Τζιώτικο Ραβαΐσι, μέρος β', (κωμῳδ. Τζώρτζου) . 1.00
7024 Καραγκιόζης, ὁ Μπάρμπα Γιώργος εἰς 'Αθήνας.—Διάλογος Μπάρμπα Γιώργου καὶ Καραγκιόζη 1.00
7025 Διάλογος Μπάρμπα Γιώργου, 'Ιταλοῦ καὶ Μπέη.—Ταβέρνα τοῦ Καραγκιόζη. (Χ. Σύλλα), ... 1.00

PANHELLENION PHONOGRAPH RECORD CO., INC.

152 West 14th Street NEW YORK, N. Y.

ΖΗΤΟΥΝΤΑΙ ΑΝΤΙΠΡΟΣΩΠΟΙ ΠΑΝΤΑΧΟΥ

Advertisement for the records of Madame Koula, owner of the Panhellenion Phonograph Record Company in New York, in the Greek-language newspaper *Atlantis*, New York, December 15, 1921

The annual picnic of the Pan-Lesbian Sappho Association at Saugus, Massachusetts, featuring Ottoman Greek musicians from the island of Lesvos and the Asia Minor coast, August 1, 1926. (Used by permission of the family of Konstantinos N. Kereakoglou)

Gus Doussas, "To Kalogeraki," *rembetiko*. Columbia Records.
G. Gretsi and S. Stamou, "Hanoumiko," Turkish dance. Greek Record Company.
G. Katsaros, "The Tavern and the Dice," *zeibekiko*. Victor Records.
Koula, "Mariori is Getting Married." Panhellenion Phonograph Record Company.
78-rpm records. (Personal collection of Christopher C. King)

Select Bibliography

Andriotis, N. 2020. *Πρόσφυγες στην Ελλάδα 1821–1940: Άφιξη, περίθαλψη, αποκατάσταση* [Refugees in Greece, 1821–1940: Arrival, Care, Restitution], Athens.

Argyriadi, M. 1991. *Η κούκλα στην ελληνική ζωή και τέχνη: Από την αρχαιότητα μέχρι σήμερα* [The Doll in Greek Life and Art: From Antiquity to the Present], Athens.

Barrs, E. B. 2020. "Marketing the Golden Rule: Near East Relief and Philanthropy's Role in the Political Economy, 1915–1930" (M.A. thesis, Univ. of Montana).

Barry, G. C. 1919. *Relief Work Among the Villages of Mount Pangaeon*, Athens.

Barton, J. L. 1930. *Story of the Near East Relief (1915–1930): An Interpretation*, New York.

Black, C. E. 1919. *Survey of the Hospitals of Greece*, Athens.

Capps, E. 1919. *The American Red Cross in Greece*, Athens.

Cassimatis, L. P. 1988. *American Influence in Greece, 1917–1929*, Kent, Ohio.

Chekimoglou, E. 2014. *Υδάτινη ιστοριογραφία: Χρονικό της διαχείρισης του νερού στην Αττική*, [Watery Historiography: Chronicle of the Management of Water in Attica], Athens.

Compton, C. C. 2008. *The Morning Cometh: 45 Years with Anatolia College, Supplemented by Carl Compton's UNRRA Letters to His Wife Ruth*, Athens.

Daleziou, E. 2013. "'Adjuster and Negotiator': Bert Hodge Hill and the Greek Refugee Crisis, 1918–1928," in *Philhellenism, Philanthropy, or Political Convenience?* (*Hesperia* 82.1), ed. J. L. Davis and N. Vogeikoff-Brogan, pp. 49–65.

Davis, J. L. 2013. "The American School of Classical Studies and the Politics of Volunteerism," in *Philhellenism, Philanthropy, or Political Convenience?* (*Hesperia* 82.1), ed. J. L. Davis and N. Vogeikoff-Brogan, pp. 15–48.

Eddy, C. B. 1931. *Greece and the Greek Refugees*, London.

Fourlis, K., ed. 1997. *Χριστιανική Αδελφότητα των Νέων Θεσσαλονίκης 1921–1996: 75 χρόνια αγάπης και κοινωνικής προσφοράς* [Young Men's Christian Association of Thessaloniki, 1921–1996: 75 Years of Love and Social Contribution], Thessaloniki.

Hajimihali, A. 1930. "Embroideries and Hand-Woven Materials: Sample-Book," in *Greek Arts and Crafts* 1, Athens.

Hajimihali, A. 1937. *L'art populaire grec*, Athens.

Hofman, H. A. 2014. "A Preliminary Visual Assessment of the Near East Relief Posters," *Journal of the Society for Armenian Studies* 23, pp. 113–136.

Horton, G. 1926. *The Blight of Asia*, Indianapolis.

Irwin, J. F. 2013. *Making the World Safe: The American Red Cross and a Nation's Humanitarian Awakening*, Oxford.

Kaika, M. 2006. "Dams as Symbols of Modernization: The Urbanization of Nature Between Geographical Imagination and Materiality," *Annals of the Association of American Geographers* 96.2, pp. 276–301.

Kalliga, C. A., ed. 2004. *Το Γεννάδειον: Δημιουργία και μεταμορφώσεις* [The Gennadeion: Creation and Transformations], Athens.

Komninou, E. 2022. *Ελένη απ' τ' Αϊβαλί: Πορεία μιας ζωής* [Eleni from Ayvali: A Course of Life], Athens.

Kontogiorgi. E. 2006. *Population Exchange in Greek Macedonia: The Rural Settlement of Refugees 1922–1930*, Oxford.

Lamb, I., and C. Lamb. 2022. *The Gentle American: George Horton's Odyssey and His True Account of the Smyrna Catastrophe*, Piscataway, N.J.

League, P. 2016. "Genealogies of Sense and Sound: Home Recordings and Greek American Identity," *Journal of Greek Media & Culture* 2.1, pp. 29–47.

League, P. 2021. *Echoes of the Great Catastrophe. Re-Sounding Anatolian Greekness in Diaspora*, Ann Arbor.

League of Nations. 1926. *Greek Refugee Settlement*, Geneva.

Lovejoy, E. P. 1933. *Certain Samaritans*, New York.

Marder, B. L. 2004. *Stewards of the Land: The American Farm School and Greece in the Twentieth Century*, Macon, Ga.

Mavrogordatos, G. T. 2017. *Μετά το 1922: Η παράταση του Διχασμού* [After 1922: The Prolongation of the National Schism], Athens.

McGrew, W. 2015. *Educating Across Cultures: Anatolia College in Turkey and Greece*, Lanham, Md.

Morgenthau, H. 1929. *I Was Sent to Athens*, New York.

Distribution of food and clothes by the ARC on the island of Oinousses near Chios, 1919. (Newberry Library, Chicago, Horace S. Oakley Papers)

Oakley, H. S. 1920. *In Macedonia*, Chicago.

Papadimas, V. 2021. *ΧΑΝΘ: Εκατό χρόνια από την ίδρυσή της. Σκέψεις - εμπειρίες - αναμνήσεις* [YMCA of Thessaloniki: A Hundred Years from Its Foundation. Thoughts - Experiences - Memories], Thessaloniki.

Piana, F. 2020. "Maternalism and Feminism in Medical Aid: The American Women's Hospitals in the United States and in Greece, 1917–1941," in *Gendering Global Humanitarianism in the Twentieth Century: Practice, Politics and the Power of Representation*, ed. E. Möller, J. Paulmann, and K. Stornig, London, pp. 85–114.

Robinson, B. A. 2013. "Hydraulic Euergetism: American Archaeology and Waterworks in Early-20th-Century Greece," in *Philhellenism, Philanthropy, or Political Convenience?* (*Hesperia* 82.1), ed. J. L. Davis and N. Vogeikoff-Brogan, pp. 15–48.